Creativity
& Writing Skills

Creativity & Writing Skills

Finding a Balance in the Primary Classroom

Kay Hiatt and Jonathan Rooke

David Fulton Publishers

London

David Fulton Publishers Ltd
414 Chiswick High Road, London W4 5TF

www.fultonpublishers.co.uk

First published in Great Britain in 2002 by David Fulton Publishers
10 9 8 7 6 5 4 3 2

British Library Cataloguing in Publication Data
A catalogue record for this book is available from the British Library.

ISBN 1–85346–787–1

Typeset by FiSH Books, London
Printed in Great Britain by The Thanet Press, Margate

Contents

Acknowledgements

Thanks to the staff and pupils of the following schools for their valuable support in the writing of this book:

- Oliver's Battery Primary School
- Selborne C of E (Aided) Primary School
- Chawton C of E (C) Primary School

Thanks also to Olga and David for their continuous support throughout the writing of this book.

'Don't call alligator long-mouth till you cross river', from *Say it Again, Granny!* by John Agard, published by The Bodley Head. Reprinted by permission of The Random House Group Ltd.

Extracts from 'The Sea Piper' by Helen Cresswell, reproduced by permission of Hodder and Stoughton Limited.

'Leaf' (1998) by John Kitching, reprinted with permission of the author; published in a Big Book anthology: *Poetry Anthology 2 'Windspells, Rainspells'*, collected by Judith Nicholls. GINN.

Extracts from Elizabeth Laird's *Secret Friends* (Hodder, 1996).

Blitz: The Diary of Edie Benson, London 1940–41, by Vince Cross (Scholastic, 2001).

'Pokemon snatch', *The Guardian*, 31 May 2000.

Chapter 1

Getting to the point of writing

At the moment of writing children are struggling to bring together a clutch of different skills, which, when working together harmoniously, will result in a piece of written work. For most children, most of the time, the act of writing is less about an artistic encounter and more about a practical and rather complicated process of construction.

Filling a blank piece of paper with words that say something worthwhile is like working on a construction site. No single builder builds a house. Instead, a combination of architects, bricklayers, surveyors, carpenters, electricians and a host of others bring to the site separate skills they have learned and integrate them. Many skills are brought together in one place, working to a plan for a specific purpose.

Starting with the foundation: young writers at Key Stage 1

Every house needs a firm foundation. Our youngest writers need many opportunities to experiment as writers in order to lay a secure foundation – they need to 'test the ground' to find out what works. Frequent opportunities to make meaning for a real purpose, which are watched and encouraged by sympathetic and informed adults, help children to understand what writing is for and become willing and eager to represent meaning on paper even before they can form letters accurately – via pictures and/or 'mark-making'. They will benefit greatly from watching adults writing in front of them and, quite often, scribing for them so that they get the idea that the spoken word can be written in a graphic form. Every aspect of writing is cemented by one type of mortar: **talk**.

By the beginning of the Reception Year children should have had many more opportunities to write, leading to a notion of sentences and coherent text structure as they move through Years 1 and 2. These skills of connecting words and sentences are rather like the bricklayer learning to set the bricks correctly in the cement in order to construct the wall – they learn from doing first and develop the finer points, i.e. which brick to choose and which angle to set it at, as they become more skilled up. The finer points of bricklaying are equivalent to word choices, sentence length, punctuation for effect and choosing from a range of connectives to move the text along as a cohesive product – which will hold the construction together. The apprentice bricklayer also needs to watch an expert at work – just as apprentice writers need to see the teacher demonstrating the finer points of writing, in front of them, and see it frequently.

Working towards completion: writers at Key Stage 2

The mind of a junior writer is something like a noisy construction site. Skills of spelling and handwriting work alongside vocabulary choice, sentence construction, paragraphing and organisation of the whole text. Each of these skills can be challenging in itself, and it must be even more daunting to deploy them all at the same time. Internal conversations are going on where decisions about each word and line are being made and adjustments debated and argued over. The quality of the child's composition depends upon the quality of this internal dialogue about what to use and how everything should be put together.

In this metaphor, then, the teacher is cast in the role of a kind of site foreman, a jack-of-all-trades, guiding the apprentice writers to take short steps to develop each of the skills they need (e.g. sentence construction and spelling) and helping them to see how to make these skills work together so they support and reinforce one another. The teacher both stimulates the imagination and creative impulses and passes on practical techniques.

What works across Key Stages 1 and 2

The setting in the Foundation Stage and the classroom in the literacy hour should become a vibrant 'writing construction site' where teachers develop four key approaches to the teaching and learning of writing:

1. **Talking:** children engage in a lot of talking about writing before writing, during writing and after writing.
2. **Stimulating:** children have a clear sense of the audience and the purpose of their writing, and have some experiences to draw on so they have something to say.
3. **Showing how:** teachers explicitly show how to write by writing in front of them and drawing their attention to specific writing techniques and how they can apply them in their own writing.
4. **Returning and reviewing:** when children can read back a text they have written, children and teachers return to the writing, inspecting it and considering what needs to be done to improve it or to move on to a greater level of dexterity.

The basic principle is that the talk around writing that goes on collectively in the classroom will provide a model for the type of internal dialogue that needs to go on in children's own minds as they write individually.

Teachers should find their practice enriched by using the ideas described in this chapter and illustrated in the classroom 'snapshots' throughout the book. Teachers not using a daily literacy hour will find the approaches and ideas equally useful for helping them to develop and sustain stimulating and structured writing lessons.

The remainder of this chapter outlines three key aspects of teaching writing. Talk for writing is threaded through each of them. These aspects are:

- stimulating their interest;
- showing them how;
- returning and reviewing.

Stimulating their interest

In fiction, poetry and non-fiction writing children need to be interested in what they are writing about if they are going to write well. Children need to have something to say. They need to be stimulated.

Concrete sources for writing: non-fiction text types

- **Other curriculum areas.** All the other subject areas provide fodder for writing. The Foundation Stage offers many chances to write non-fiction linked to the play area: labels, lists, notices etc. From Year R onwards the learning that takes place is usually assessed through writing of some kind. The texts they need to write in other subject areas must be taught as part of the literacy strategy. A rich source in many primary schools is content from PE and maths lessons, e.g. writing instructions for a new game using balls and hoops, organising and presenting findings using precise mathematical language and vocabulary, such as drawing conclusions from statistics and graphs.
- **School visits.** A wide variety of visits take place, from supermarkets to the seaside, from museums to battleships. Plan what the focus for writing will be beforehand and show the children how to make simple notes, allow them to take photos, perhaps using a digital camera, feed them with questions and observations that get them thinking and talking about what they see – all this instead of the dreaded worksheet which they have to fill in as evidence of learning.
- **Visits from outsiders to the school.** Use parents, governors and other teachers in the school who have a wealth of skills and experience to use as a basis for writing – from the long-distance lorry driver to the freelance writer, from the deep sea diver to the trainee teacher. Borrow a member of a history re-enactment group or use the museum service, which often uses actors 'in role', e.g. a Victorian head teacher.
- **The local area.** Focused 'walk-abouts' give children real things to write about. In the Foundation Stage this could be a walk to talk about the print they see around them and to photograph it, and to put up a display in school – who is it for and what is the purpose? In Year 6 it may be for a piece of compare and contrast writing based on the local mosque and church.
- **Objects and artefacts brought into the school.** Objects borrowed from museums and school services, such as a selection of fossils, farming implements, Second World War photographs or an old census, can stimulate different genres of writing.
- **Drama.** Use hot-seating, children in role, improvised conversations and freeze frames for a key moment in a historical event. All of these give the children another experience, a different way into thinking about what they will write. Use mime for the different stages of a process in science or geography and ask children to write captions for the stages.

Stimulation for poetry

Experience is the key factor in stimulating poetry and fiction writing. Children are more likely to enjoy writing poetry if it is about something they have experienced. More authentic and vigorous writing is likely to emerge if children are asked to craft a poem about something they know well and have experienced with their own senses, e.g. having their hair cut, the playground, getting ready to go to sleep – even sitting SAT examinations! Use the following:

- **Artefacts** that can be closely observed, touched and smelled, engaging the senses.
- **Observational drawings**, where details are seen, dwelt on and thought about.
- **School visits**, which can provide material for poems.
- **Other curriculum areas.** Work undertaken in other areas of the curriculum can frequently stimulate poetry writing. The work done in a nature area or on light can provide material for poems, e.g. a list poem at Year 1.
- **Published poems.** Giving pupils time to read a variety of published poems can trigger new poems they would never have thought of writing.
- **Drama.** Rehearsing for a piece of role play, e.g. Mrs Fox underground in fear for her life (from *Fantastic Mr Fox* by Roald Dahl), can lead to a poem rather than prose at Year 2.
- **Guided reading**, where children are exploring motives of characters and themes of books, e.g. Blitz by Vince Cross, can lead to poetry on war and evacuation at Year 6.

The key is that children have something to base their poems on.

Writing stories

Most parents are aware of the importance of books in their young children's lives, and the most familiar genre is the story. (See Appendix 1, Involving parents at Foundation Stage and Key Stage 1.) As well as offering enormous pleasure and fun for both parent and child, the reading aloud of books enables children to learn about the features and organisation of language. The way in which parents read books is important too, and they should use their voices to effect, attending to the punctuation to help meaning and express the emotions of the characters. Reading stories aloud and storytelling are crucial throughout Key Stages 1 and 2 – reading and listening leads to telling and writing.

The National Literacy Strategy has built into its objectives the importance of retelling stories and this can be accomplished in innovative ways, e.g. 'in the round' as a whole class and in small groups. The teacher can stop the story at any time and scribe for the class the last sentence, using the whole range of print conventions to express meaning, e.g. big bold letters for shouting. Many children at Key Stage 1 may still be unaware of how print can convey the spoken word, through lack of experience of sharing books at home.

Retelling also allows the creation of mind maps of a story, useful scaffolds which children can internalise and use in their own story writing.

Using fairy stories and other well known classes of stories as models for writing gives the children a further kick-start into writing in genre.

At Key Stage 2, writing stories will involve drawing on ideas from, among other things, personal experience, the experiences of friends and relations heard in anecdotes, books read, films and television seen, places visited, feelings experienced and people known.

By bringing in artefacts, telling stories, recalling places we have been and how we have felt at particular times, drawing attention to features of professional authors' work and using drama and video we can begin to stimulate children's story writing.

How audience and purpose engage children in the act of writing

Having an audience for writing and knowing its purpose is a tremendous stimulus for writing. The 'snapshots' in this book give you many examples of this in action. The audience may be imaginary – e.g. writing a postcard to the Big Bad Wolf in Year 1 or to a local council arguing persuasively for Danny (from *Danny Champion of the World* by Roald Dahl) not to be taken into care – but the purpose is the same: to persuade someone to agree with their views in Year 6. The role of the teacher in encouraging children to write in this way is crucial if we want writers to be interested in what they are doing.

Finding ways of publishing writing as often as possible remains today, in the era of the National Literacy Strategy, as important as it ever was and, indeed, it is strongly recommended by the strategy.

Attractively presented books of children's own poems, stories and non-fiction are always impressive. They speak volumes about the value and prestige given to the hard work of writing and children take pride in the books.

Poetry is an oral experience and poems written for performance should be performed by the writers. This can happen in an assembly, at a grand poetry evening to which parents are invited, on a poetry soapbox placed in a convenient spot in the playground at playtime or on a video.

Plays can be performed and videoed and then presented to the school on 'the big screen' at a lunchtime 'cinema' by playing the videotape through a PowerPoint projector. The playwrights can form a panel and be briefly questioned by the audience afterwards. The same thing could be done as 'live theatre'.

Poems and extracts from stories from across the school can be included in regular newsletters that go home to the parents or in school newspapers, or placed in a frame outside the reception window and given the accolade 'writing of the week'. Each year a 'writing yearbook' with many poems and extracts can be produced, printed and then sold to children and parents to cover the costs.

Letters and e-mails can be sent to children in other schools both in Britain and abroad, depending on the quality of the links the school has. Whole projects and displays about the school and the local area can be exchanged. A very motivating idea in one school involved the children having to create a portfolio of work on their local area and send it to children in a school in a contrasting area of the country to try to persuade them to move there.

These kinds of things take time and require a commitment from the whole staff, but they do provide audiences, who in turn provide responses to children's writing, and responses to writing provide motivation and stimulation – they are a reward for the hard work involved in writing. They are even fun!

A culture of writing can be created in school where all forms of writing are valued. With this whole-school effort to raise the profile and prestige of writing, all pupils' standards of writing are likely to be pulled up. Without this type of culture, other efforts to raise standards are less likely to succeed as well as they might.

Showing them how

Providing a stimulus for writing is one half of the equation, but showing children how to write is the other. With both running side by side there will be an improvement in writing. The 'snapshots' throughout the book give examples of this.

Writing in front of the children, or shared writing as it is called in the National Literacy Strategy, allows children to see and hear how a more experienced writer (the teacher) would struggle with constructing the text. This is a bit like attaching a microphone to a footballer and asking him to play football and broadcast the football commentary at the same time. It involves two skills: the ability to write in a particular way and the ability to explain the techniques you are using. It also requires the ability to control and involve the children. So before the children leave for their desks to write on their own, the teacher is effectively saying, 'Hold on. Sit down and I'll show you how I would do it and then you can use some of the approaches I show you. I will slow the process down and let you in on what I am thinking about as I write.'

Shared writing in the National Literacy Strategy

Shared writing is the pivotal point in the teaching of writing in the National Literacy Strategy. It should always be driven by specific learning objectives, which are shared with the children each lesson. The approach is illustrated in the model below, drawn from NLS training materials.

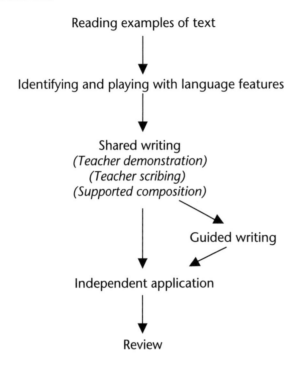

The reading and analysis of texts that precede shared writing, as well as interactive lessons on aspects of grammar, e.g. adverbs, lead up to and feed into the shared writing lesson. In the same way, all the independent writing and guided writing that follows hangs on the quality of teaching and the expectations established in the shared writing.

Teacher demonstration is when the teacher writes in front of the children and they watch and listen. The teacher is not to be interrupted and is giving a sort of performance, while the children take on the role of a kind of audience.

Teacher scribing is when the children are more directly involved and asked to think of the next line or next part of the composition, and then to tell the teacher, who decides which ideas to use, explaining the reasons for her choice, and then writes them on the board.

Supported composition is when the children work together in pairs to write the next part of the composition.

The most effective learning is likely to take place in a shared writing lesson where the children are actively involved. It is unlikely that many classes are going to watch a teacher modelling the process of writing for very long before some either quietly switch off or begin to distract others. The best way to retain attention and maximise the children's involvement in the learning is to use a combination of the three parts of shared writing described above. You might start with some demonstration and then ask the children to write down the next line on their hand-held whiteboards (show-me boards) or in their exercise books, and then discuss and demonstrate more, and so on.

Show-me boards – A4-sized write-on/wipe-off boards – have proved to be extremely useful tools. They work well for a number of reasons. Children respond well to them because they do not carry the threat of permanence. The children can wipe away any errors

6

or make space for changes and additions to their sentences, and this encourages exploratory writing behaviour. The boards are firm enough to be used on the mat and large enough for pairs of children to work together, and this encourages the type of talk you want to develop. As the children hold up their boards for the teacher to see, the teaching assistant can be asked to focus on particular children's writing as a form of assessment.

Writing 'live': shared writing

It may seem uncomfortable to put ourselves in a position where we may at times be struggling in front of our class, but from the children's perspective it is far more helpful to see and hear how a writer overcomes problems similar to those they themselves may be encountering. It is always a relief to know that other people have the same problems as they have with writing, and it moves children forward to see the way those problems are overcome.

An effective shared writing session will often have two key objectives:

• teaching a set of writing skills that are generic and can be applied to all the children's writing tasks across the whole curriculum;
• a specific technique or skill that the children are expected to apply in their own writing as a result of the shared writing.

Generic writing skills

If we were to slow down what happens in our heads when we write it might look something like this:

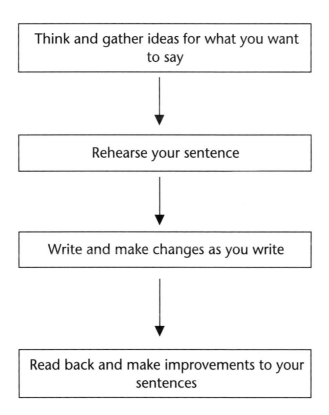

This model applies to a wide range of writing, including letters, stories, poems and reports. Experienced writers do these things whenever they write. Sometimes it happens very quickly; at other times the process is long and drawn out. The 'snapshots' in this book allow you to zoom into classrooms to see this happening at first hand. It is crucial that this is happening throughout Key Stages 1 and 2 so that we enable children to move from the speakerly writing that they use at first when they write recounts to the writerly writing they must use for the range of writing genres required in school.

As you demonstrate in front of them look for opportunities to:

- add words;
- remove words;
- replace words;
- move words to another place in the sentence;
- change the clause structure;
- move sentences to other places in the paragraph;
- make new paragraph breaks;
- adjust the tense so that it is consistent;
- make spelling corrections;
- celebrate words and sentences that work well.

Of course, you would select only some of these to emphasise in each writing lesson, but over time children will begin to see how these techniques improve the quality of their writing. It is like a potter who makes the pot and shaves off some clay here, adds a bit there and pushes it a bit here with her fingers. Most children have made pots with plasticine or clay and they will respond to this simile.

Talk is clearly a major feature of shared writing. Writing in this model is anything but a solitary activity. It is a collaborative learning experience where children are clearly learning from one another, being given the opportunity to achieve with other people what they could not achieve on their own.

Teaching children to use a variety of sentences

Children will be able to express themselves clearly and have control over their writing when they are able to manipulate sentences. It is not the ability to write long sentences that defines a good writer. It is the ability to deploy a variety of sentences appropriately in writing that is the mark of a competent writer. New materials produced for teachers – *Developing Early Writing for Key Stage 1* and *Grammar for Writing for Key Stage 2* – take teachers through this approach to grammar in a logical and helpful way.

The golden rules of shared writing

Shared writing is an enjoyable and interesting aspect of teaching children to write. It is worth devising a set of criteria against which to evaluate how well your lessons are going and to identify areas for personal development. Below is a 'personal checklist' compiled and adapted from comments made by teachers on shared writing training courses when they were asked to identify what sort of things they would see and hear in an effective shared writing lesson. All these points can be prefaced by the question 'Do I see/hear...'.

Golden Rules of Shared Writing

Do I see/hear...

- An enthusiastic teacher?
- Children taking part and interacting with the teacher?
- Children's contributions valued by the teacher, who shares and elicits their ideas?
- Children talking with each other about writing, making decisions together and actually writing themselves?
- Reading back and refining?
- Reference to aspects of writing previously learned in shared reading and sentence-level work?
- The teacher giving a running commentary and justifying choices while writing?
- Adequate time?
- A pace that responds to the needs of the children and the stage of the lesson?
- Careful and detailed planning that builds on what the children can do already in writing because of regular monitoring of written work?
- The objectives written where the children can see them?
- Learning objectives referred to explicitly and frequently throughout the lesson?

The 'snapshots' show in more detail what shared writing might sound like and what the board might look like in the classroom.

Returning and revising: looking back to move forward

As soon as children can read back a text they have written at Key Stage 1 it is time to expect that they re-read it to check for meaning. This is hard for children and they will need plenty of demonstrations on how to do it, e.g. using anonymous pieces of writing that the teacher has collected from previous years. Children in Year 2 and more able writers in Year 1 are becoming more reflective and more prepared to re-read, and it is worth teaching them how to do it. This can be done during whole-class, small group and individual sessions.

At Key Stage 2 children need dedicated time to read their writing back and make improvements. They need to learn the value of redrafting and how to redraft. Most pieces of writing across all subjects will, at most, be drafted for only a second time. Children need to be able to draft their writing:

- on their own as they are 'looping back';
- at intervals during their writing with a partner and on their own;
- at the end of a piece of writing, again both on their own and with a partner;
- with the guidance of a teacher during guided writing.

If we want children to be able to read their own and each other's work with a critical eye then we need to show them the skills of revising and editing. It is essential that children practise the habit of reading back their own work as they are writing, and do not wait until the whole composition is completed. Showing how continues throughout Key Stage 2.

Golden Rules for Editing

- Are there any words that need to be deleted?
- Are there any words that need to be added?
- Are there any words that need to be replaced?
- Are there any clauses or sentences that can be moved to a better place?
- Is the piece structured well?
- Is some of the information in the wrong paragraph?
- Are the paragraphs separated in the right place?
- Are the paragraphs introduced well?
- Are there a variety of sentence starters?
- Are there a variety of sentence types?

Providing success criteria

Don't try to apply all the 'golden rules for editing', all the time, for every piece of work. It is well worth keeping a special focus on some key aspects of writing, and these are likely to be determined by the particular objectives which have been guiding the unit of work, e.g. use of dialogue or speech verbs.

Lists on posters or small photocopied cards, to remind children of the key things they should be looking for in the particular form they have been writing, will help to guide them in their revision. An example might look like this:

Does your opening:

- Grab readers' attention and make them want to read on?
- Start with something more interesting than 'once upon a time'?
- Set the scene by including a setting?
- Describe the main character?
- Perhaps start with dialogue?

Posters like this will be more effective if the children are involved in deciding what is included on it and the poster is written up as the children are taught about the genre of non-fiction writing, the form of poetry or the elements of a story.

Reviewing each other's writing

It seems that when children read their work to **someone else** the ways to revise and improve their writing become clearer. The comments they hear other members of their own class make about their work may have a greater impact than any written comments from a teacher. Comments made during drafting can also be acted upon immediately – marking is unlikely to lead to any changes in the work it is written on and may well be forgotten.

A way of helping children to develop skills of peer evaluation is to produce a review sheet that the children can fill in together. What is important is that the children's critical drafting skills are developed, and they are gradually being trained in how to do the same activity independently without the guidance sheet.

The example guidance sheet can be used with more able children or children in the upper junior years. It encourages the children to reflect on their own writing and that of others, and demands that the children identify and celebrate the positive aspects of their writing.

Date	
Name of author	Name of drafting buddy
Title of writing	
What I was trying to achieve	
What I did well	
What I think I need to change	
Drafting buddy's comments – what works and how writing could be improved	
Things to do to improve my writing • •	
Signed	Signed

Children do not have to write down their comments. Reflection and analysis of their writing in peer groups can be equally if not more useful to them if done orally with a card or poster to guide their discussion. They need to be shown how to engage in this type of dialogue by the teacher and receive explicit instruction in the skills of speaking and listening. Asking themselves how well they participated in this type of drafting dialogue and how to improve their performance would be a useful exercise in itself.

Guided writing: spotlight on the reading process

If shared writing with a whole class of children with varying abilities and at different stages of writing development is opening a window on to the writing process, then working with a small group of children of roughly the same ability in guided writing is putting a spotlight on writing.

Guided writing provides the space for personal discussion about children's writing to take place in a busy classroom.

What happens in a guided writing session?

Guided writing sessions usually involve a group of no more than six children sitting around a table with their teacher. The children may have their exercise books with them or copies of some writing they have recently done. They may be looking at photocopies of another child's work or they may be writing on handheld whiteboards (show-me boards). Sessions usually last for around 20 minutes in junior classrooms.

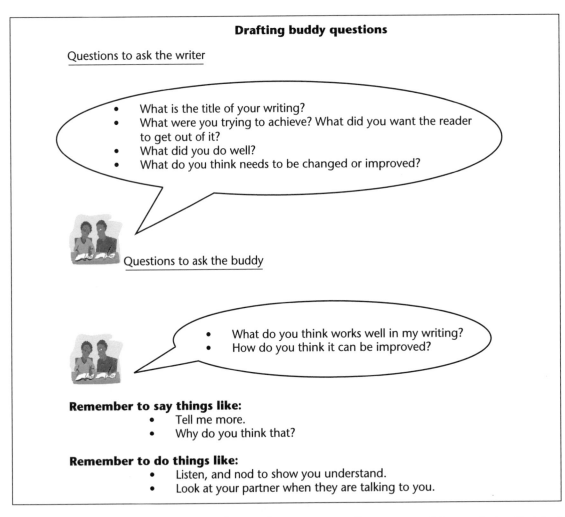

Drafting buddy questions

Questions to ask the writer

- What is the title of your writing?
- What were you trying to achieve? What did you want the reader to get out of it?
- What did you do well?
- What do you think needs to be changed or improved?

Questions to ask the buddy

- What do you think works well in my writing?
- How do you think it can be improved?

Remember to say things like:
- Tell me more.
- Why do you think that?

Remember to do things like:
- Listen, and nod to show you understand.
- Look at your partner when they are talking to you.

Any shorter time is often felt to be inadequate to make any teaching points. Guided writing sessions can be held during the 20-minute slot for independent work in the literacy hour or can be held at any other time in the day. An obvious opportunity for guided writing is when children are writing a report, acccount or other genre during history, science, geography etc.

Guided writing sessions are used at different stages in the writing process.

Before writing

Teachers can help a group of children to develop skills in planning their writing. This might take the form of a mini shared writing session where the children work together, discussing a plan for a story that the teacher 'scribes' on a flip chart, which has been moved to the guided writing desk. A useful and mobile alternative is a large kitchen whiteboard which can be carried to the desk and supported on the teacher's knee. The children may already have written plans and they work together on one of the children's plans to develop it.

During writing

This is perhaps one of the most exciting opportunities guided writing offers. Children can focus on a writing skill such as describing a character or taking notes and writing a paragraph. Using hand-held whiteboards and dry-wipe pens the children write sentences either on their own or in pairs. The children may have seen the teacher demonstrate writing a character sketch and now the teacher watches and assists them in writing their own. She might ask them to share ideas about their character, think of useful vocabulary, rehearse a sentence, remind them of some key skills and then watch them as they write on whiteboards. Teachers have the opportunity to intervene and make suggestions at the point of composition as the children are writing or when they have finished. An observer might hear the teacher make comments like: 'Why are you using that word?', 'Can you start the sentence with a better word?', 'I think that is very effective', 'Are you sure that is what you want to say?', 'Can you write these two sentences so that they make one longer sentence?' 'Why not move this clause here?'

The children can then be urged to read their sentences back to themselves and then to each other, and to make changes. While the teacher is watching the children write, she will be making mental notes of what to comment on when the sentences are reviewed as a group. After the children have commented on each other's work the teacher, holding up the children's whiteboards so everyone can see, can say what she was impressed with. The sorts of things might be:

- I was impressed with the way Philip quietly read back that first line to himself and then replaced the verb 'walked' with 'trudged'. Tell me why you changed the word, Phil.
- Edward has used something interesting. Look at this star at the bottom here with a sentence next to it and this star in the middle of this paragraph. Is this sentence to add in? Why did you want to add this? Where did you get the idea of using a star to indicate a new line to be inserted?
- Maria has really got the idea of using a subordinate clause. Does it work?

What is interesting about this sort of intense guided writing session is that while the teacher is offering ideas on how to improve one child's writing, other children can be seen hastily changing what they have written to do something similar.

After writing

This is perhaps most effective when children have already started a piece of writing. The teacher reads through the work that has been written so far and selects some children to work with the next lesson. She identifies and prepares some key revisions to make when they draft in the guided writing session. It is important that all the children in the group can see a copy of the writing they are going to work on. Three photocopies should be sufficient so that pairs of children can share. It is difficult to remember and work on a piece of writing that is read out loud but not seen, and this does not allow the children to practise their skills of editing and revision so they can independently apply these same skills to their own writing.

Then with their partner they make any changes to the text using a contrasting coloured pen. The group then discuss what works well and why and how the writing could be improved. Ideas will be proposed, tested, discarded or built upon by all the members of the group. In many ways, the type of talk will be similar to that described above. The children work together to make one child's writing better than he could have made it on his own and they learn from each other in the process. It is collaborative learning, and writing becomes something you do with others. In some ways it resembles guided reading in that the children are approaching the text as both readers and writers. It is a powerful way of learning about writing for an audience.

You can focus attention by writing one sentence under discussion on to a larger whiteboard where the vocabulary and structure can really be put under a microscope and operated on by the children to make it stronger and more effective.

There is not time to dwell too long on each child, so a targeted point or two made about each piece of work will maintain a stimulating pace and retain interest. Sometimes, it is better to have smaller groups for this work as it means you can give more quality time to a composition if it needs it.

The child whose work is shown in Figure 1.1 is an able writer who has just started Year 3. She reads a lot. In this story she is using a lot of descriptive vocabulary and some interesting language devices, such as the simile 'like a mouse against a sea monster'. She does not yet read back with the eyes and ears of a reader.

<u>Teddy gets lost!</u>

One sunny morning I drowsily set off in my shiny speedboat with tiny teddy and cheese sand-wiches. We went zooming through the glistening blue & green waves crashing together like the battle of waterloo. Suddenly a [*viscious*] tremendously big wave towered over my little speed boat, like a mouse against a sea-monster. I broke the foamy spray and skimmed over the battle, glimpsing at all the little sea horses trailing behind the smart soldiers, waiting to battle the enemies' troops. An unexpected faint trumpeting noise sounded, [*as*] the troops approached each other. [*because*] the battle had started ! My eyes started to burn, all the vibrant colours were frying me. My eyes could stand it no longer my fists clenched together I wanted teddy but, all I could find was cheese were was teddy. I'm hungry I thought, here are my sand wiches [*I couldn't believe it. I had packed Teddy in my sand wiches.*] Yuck teddy Sand wiches! Teddy you're back! I love you Ugh you're smeared in butter. Oh well I don't mind lets take you home and get you cleaned up I sailed back not [*Smiling to myself,*] through a battle but a gentle calm lullaby instead . That night I slept like sleep does itself.

Figure 1.1

During the guided writing session the teacher had three objectives. The young writer needed to **read back** the sentence 'An unexpected, faint trumpeting…battle had started.' Once this was done the other members of the group said that it was a little confusing. The teacher guided the way she could reorganise the longer sentence into two shorter sentences by using the conjunction 'as' and making a short sentence for impact: 'The battle had started.' It was suggested that 'faint' may not be an effective adjective and she chose to delete it. On reading back the next sentence she realised that the insertion of the conjunction or 'gluing word' 'because' would improve the quality of her sentence and make the meaning clearer.

The same problem was addressed further down the story, where she finds the lost teddy in her sandwiches. While it was clear in her mind what was happening, other readers were confused. With the help of the teacher and the group new sentences were constructed and inserted into the paragraph.

Finally, the teacher wanted to begin to develop the repertoire of sentences she could use and suggested she begin a sentence with 'Smiling to myself…'. She tells the child that you can start sentences with these words ending in -ing and they can be quite effective. It is something they can work on together during the year.

The teacher realises that perhaps one of the next steps for this child is to work on setting out and composing dialogue.

There are probably too many points made on this story for one writing session, and it would be better to just focus on one or two. However, this gives an idea of the range of points that can be taught in guided writing with a more able child.

Figure 1.2 is an extract from the work of a Year 4 boy who is enthusiastic about his writing and responds well to suggestions to help him progress. He has written a story and the teacher praises the many positive points. She chooses one section of it to discuss with the group, and targets two main points – considering the needs of the reader and devices to build up tension.

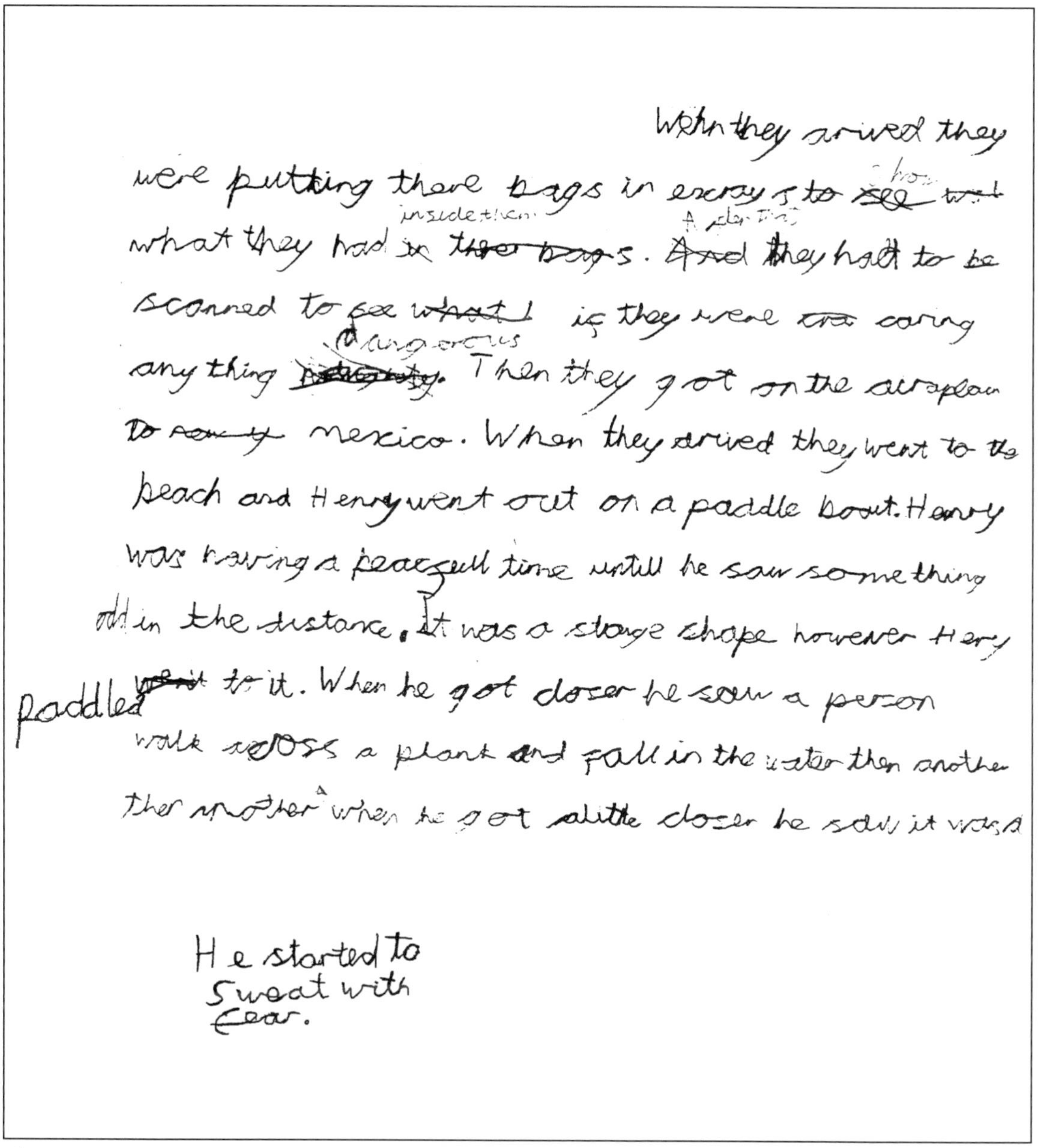
When they arived they were putting there bags in exray's to show what they had inside them. A plan. They had to be scanned to see if they were carring any thing dangerous. Then they got on the aeroplane To mexico. When they arived they went to the beach and Henry went out on a paddle boat. Henry was having a peaceful time untill he saw something odd in the distance. It was a strange shape however Henry paddled to it. When he got closer he saw a person walk across a plank and fall in the water then another then another when he got a little closer he saw it was a

He started to sweat with fear.

Figure 1.2

The boy enjoys reading out the extract to the group and it becomes apparent to him that the first two sentences are a little confusing for the reader and need to be tidied up.

Two words are replaced with 'show' and 'inside them'. The word 'And' is replaced with a time connective. The word 'naughty' doesn't seem quite right, so the group come up with the idea of 'dangerous'.

The teacher praises his use of time connectives to help the narrative run smoothly and his effective use of 'until'. She also points out how well he has begun to build up tension and suggests they work on it together to put in some new words and a short sentence that will heighten the tension in the reader. They decide to add the word 'odd' and replace 'went' with 'paddle' – a more powerful verb. Finally, they insert a short sharp sentence to say how Henry felt as he approached this peculiar plank.

Not all these points need to be made in a single guided writing session and it may not be worthwhile asking the child to rewrite the story neatly – the learning has taken place during the session. The boy has had his writing taken seriously and the teacher has focused his attention on the challenging business of sentence construction.

Figure 1.3 is from a Year 4 boy who has been writing a story. In the guided writing session the teacher decides to focus on the way he has overused short sentences and to help him to join some of the information together so that he can use a variety of sentences. First, the teacher praises his choice of vocabulary and his very story-like sentence 'Out came a silver box'. The children all agree it is a very interesting piece of writing.

Bobs mum closed the door. Bobs mum took the box into the kitchen. Bob followed her. He peeped round the door. His mum teared the package open. Out came a silver box. Bob hid in a pile of sacks.

His mum left the silver box on the Table.

Figure 1.3

The teacher explains that some of these sentences could be linked together using the gluing word 'and'. They decide to combine the first two sentences so that they become:

*Bobs mum closed the door **and** Bobs mum took the box into the kitchen.*

They then discuss how they do not need 'Bobs mum' to be repeated and use the pronoun 'she' instead.

*Bobs mum closed the door **and she** took the box into the kitchen.*

Then they discuss how they could use 'and he saw' to join two more sentences.

He peeped round the door and he saw his mum teared the package open.

When the group read it back they decide the tense is wrong and it should be 'tear' the package. One child suggests he use the pronoun 'her' instead of 'his mum' in this sentence.

The boy reads his writing back and the group agree it sounds better. The teacher makes a note that he does not understand the possessive apostrophe.

Showing not telling

Guided writing sessions do not always have to revolve around the children's own texts. It can involve the use of cards to help children to develop specific writing skills the teacher has identified as weak or in need of extension, e.g. using adjectives effectively, as in the example below.

Simple sentences might be presented to them on cards in the middle of the table. For example:

| The | | boy | | sat | | in | | the | | playground | | . |

The children are given blank cards and asked to write suitable adjectives on them, which are then inserted in the sentence. Their effectiveness is discussed.

| The | | scared | | boy | | sat | | in | | the | | cold | | playground | | . |

They can then be given simple sentences and asked to choose descriptive words to make them richer and write them on their whiteboards. Of course, this sort of lesson might be most effective if towards the end they were given their own sentences extracted from previous compositions to develop in the same way.

Guided writing can also be used to extend a more able group ready to be stretched by a new device or technique, e.g. using a non-finite verb at the beginning of a sentence: 'Quivering, she reached for the door.'

Things to consider when planning guided writing sessions

The questions on the guided writing tree below can be used to help you think through how you will organise guided writing sessions.

Guided writing

- offers teachers a chance to observe children as they write;
- gives the opportunity to develop children's self-esteem;
- provides a supportive and constructively critical audience for children's writing;
- links to the learning objectives for writing taught through shared reading and writing;
- creates a bridge for children between whole-class learning and applying skills and techniques independently;
- is carefully planned with a main learning objective that is shared with the children;
- is characterised by children and teachers involved in well managed collaborative talk;
- teaches children speaking and listening skills;
- stretches children because the work is closely linked to their ability;
- offers children a space to reflect on their own writing;
- offers an opportunity to help children to meet their individual or group writing targets.

Many people find organising guided writing sessions difficult at first because children from other groups tend to demand attention and there is a strong temptation to walk around the classroom fielding children's questions and offering help where needed. Teachers can also be quite tired after 30 minutes of focused whole-class teaching in the first half of the literacy hour. It is worth reminding yourself of the benefits to the children of this type of teaching, to give you the will to overcome the problems in establishing the routines within the group and among the class. Some schools have found guided writing so beneficial that they run a 20-minute session each literacy hour and find space for guided reading at another time of the day.

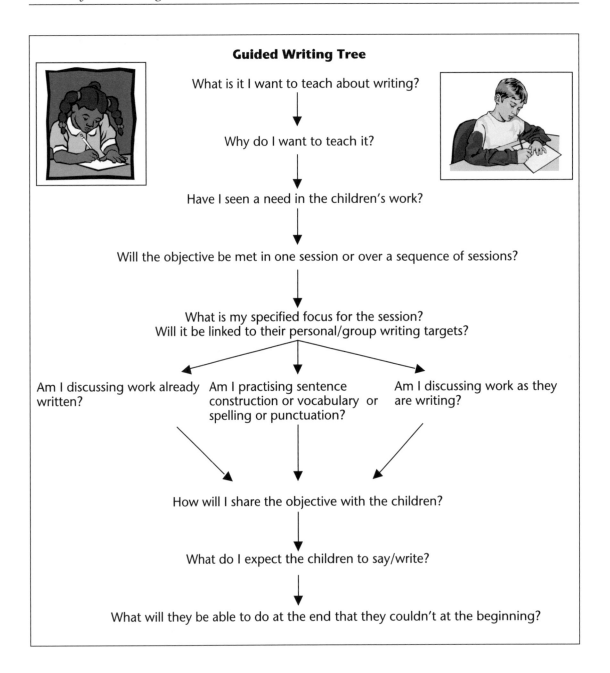

Guided Writing Tree

What is it I want to teach about writing?

↓

Why do I want to teach it?

↓

Have I seen a need in the children's work?

↓

Will the objective be met in one session or over a sequence of sessions?

↓

What is my specified focus for the session?
Will it be linked to their personal/group writing targets?

Am I discussing work already written?

Am I practising sentence construction or vocabulary or spelling or punctuation?

Am I discussing work as they are writing?

↓

How will I share the objective with the children?

↓

What do I expect the children to say/write?

↓

What will they be able to do at the end that they couldn't at the beginning?

Summary

Writing in this model is taught and learned through talking. Professional authors' work is read and discussed in the hope that imitation will lead to invention and competence. The pivotal context for talk is shared writing where children see and hear their teachers write in front of them, explaining the vocabulary choices they make, how they are forming a variety of sentences to have a particular effect on the audience and how they are sewing the sentences together to construct a text form suitable for their purpose. Writing in this model is interactive; the children are involved, making contributions and discussing them. Guided writing provides a small group context where teachers have the opportunity to work on specific objectives with a few children of roughly the same ability and take them forward.

Clear objectives gleaned from gazing into children's writing to assess what they can do and what their next step is inform carefully planned lessons which pay attention to audience, form and purpose. Efforts are made to capitalise on cross-curricular links so that the children have something to say, and creative stimuli are used to excite the children for stories and poems. The classroom in this model has a culture of risk taking, reflection and openness cultivated by the teacher, who leads from the front by taking risks and showing how to write – urging children forward but showing them how to take the necessary steps.

There is still a central place for silence and concentration when writing, but the experiences outlined in this chapter should carry over into independent writing to enable the production of an altogether more effective piece of writing.

Chapter 2

Writing at the Foundation Stage for the playgroup, nursery and reception class

In this chapter we examine: the practitioner's role; assessment; talking to young children about their writing; independent writing; moving towards book writing; handwriting; shared and demonstration writing; ICT links; oral rehearsal of writing; drama; story sacks. We cover the following texts: notices; postcards; instructions; recountings; stories.

There has been a growing awareness in recent years of the importance of building in many more opportunities for writing at the early years stage. This has featured in many Ofsted reports.

The National Literacy Strategy recommends an active role for the teacher, offering clear guidance for how to do it in materials such as *Developing Early Writing* and *Grammar for Writing*. This is also recommended in the new *Curriculum Guidance for the Foundation Stage*. See Appendix 2 for more detail on the links between both.

The purpose of this chapter is to offer ideas and detailed examples or 'snapshots' of these approaches in action with children in the early years. The 'snapshots' embrace the notion of a 'problem-solving approach', where children are engaged in and committed to the activity and see a real purpose in what they are doing. Speaking and listening underpin all the activities in writing.

The teacher/practitioner's role is crucial and they need to be up to date with the latest approaches (see Appendix 2). Teaching assistants and parents involved with young children writing need to know the typical development of young children as writers. The concept of the attentive, interested and tutoring adult is essential to bring early writing experiences up to the level of other literacy activities in the early years.

Seeking out a stimulating purpose for writing: practitioners 'in role' to support young writers

The idea of practitioners going into role is becoming increasingly popular as a way of drawing children into the play area for a real purpose. This needs to be organised by the teacher and stated in the planning. Teaching assistants can, in close liaison with the teacher, play a full, active and enjoyable role in the area.

The practitioner may be in role as:

- the hairdresser or vet showing the children how to answer the phone and then fill in an appointment slip;

- the owner of the toy shop who needs sticky labels attached to all the toys with a picture and a price;
- a customer who is filling in a complaint form about a pair of shoes she bought;
- the pilot of the hot air balloon writing a notice warning passengers to 'keep still'.

No training in drama is necessary for the practitioner to go into role, only willingness to take the role seriously and prepare for it with as much care as planning a science activity. The benefits are tremendous in that they make the writing situation come to life for the children, encouraging them to be involved and interested.

Writing and the role-play area

The role-play area has long been recognised as having a central part to play in all early learning, including the acquisition of literacy skills. Speaking and listening skills can be developed within an interesting scenario which children are drawn to. There are many links with reading and writing. Several times in the year, give the children the chance to help to plan this area; they will feel some ownership of it if they have been actively involved. Make sure that this happens by putting it into the term's planning.

Planning the role-play area together: an opportunity for demonstrating writing for a real purpose

The teacher will have a very good idea of what the role-play area will be, and will involve the children in her planning, taking on board suggestions from the children.

Group the children together and ask them questions along the following lines:

- What should it be?
- Where should it go?
- What should it look like from the outside?
- What things should go inside?
- What writing is needed?

The teacher can draw up a list from their suggestions, writing it in front of them and demonstrating that writing has a real purpose. This is left up on the wall or flip chart and referred to as the area takes shape.

The role-play area is great for supporting and developing children's speaking, listening and writing skills. Below are some examples of possible role-play areas, with links to writing (in italics) clearly made. Make some of the texts suggested below available for the children in the role-play area. Children may like to copy them on some occasions, and frequently they will have a go at 'writing' their own versions.

Writing opportunities linked to role-play areas

Services: garage, bank, post office, hairdresser, vet, dentist, doctor, hotel, café, travel agent etc.
Writing: *appointment lists, forms, message pad, order pads, menus, prescriptions, receipts.*

Shops: video shop, DIY, shoe shop, toy shop, beach shop, baby clothes shop, kitchenware shop, greetings card shop etc.
Writing: *stock list, price labels, receipts, complaint forms, free product leaflets, instructions.*

Imaginative: spaceship, pirate ship, hot air balloon, cave, castle, Santa's grotto.
Writing: *tickets, maps, message in a bottle, signs, warnings, Santa's order book.*

What follows is a variety of 'snapshots for writing' which are closely linked to the Curriculum Guidance for Early Years and the National Literacy Strategy objectives for writing at Year R (see Appendix 2).

Plotting the path through the planning

The success of the 'Lost Teddy' scenario that follows owes much to the practitioner, who is in role, demonstrating her belief that this situation could really happen. This and the following snapshots are linked to objectives taken from the new DfES curriculum guidance for the Foundation Stage.

Snapshot 1 A lost teddy

Talking through what it is you want to teach

A captive audience of young writers sit around an early years practitioner. Some are five years of age, the rest four-year-olds. In a concerned voice she shows them a teddy bear which has a label tied around its arm that reads 'I am lost – please find my owner.'

The group is concerned about this lost teddy and the teacher's sympathetic tone of voice helps the group to empathise with the teddy's plight.

They discuss possible ways of helping and she leads their discussion towards the idea of a notice – which could be fixed in the window of the early years unit. The hope is that whoever owns the teddy will read it and collect him.

Showing how to do it

Turning to a whiteboard with a sheet of A3 paper attached, she talks aloud to the children, telling them what she is going to write:

> I think we need a big heading at the top of our notice – I am going to write the heading in capital letters.

She tells them she is writing this in capital letters so that someone walking by will be able to see it quite clearly. Thinking aloud, she states that the first word in the heading will be 'FOUND', followed by what has been found. An oral rehearsal of the heading follows and then this is written up:

FOUND – ONE TEDDY BEAR

She explains why she is using a really thick pen for these words – so that they will show up. Now she continues thinking aloud for the children, saying that she must write what the bear looks like and where it was found.

She writes the following, stopping after every entry and re-reading it – the children join in if they wish to.

> **FOUND – ONE TEDDY BEAR**
> A small brown teddy bear was found this morning at the Grove Nursery.
> He was sitting near the computer.

Now I'm going to re-read this – is it what I wanted to say? Have I written what the teddy looks like? Yes. Have I written where he was found? Yes.

> If you are the owner, please come in and collect him.

Finally, I must ask the owner to come inside, if the teddy belongs to him. If you are the owner, please come in and collect him.

> **FOUND – ONE TEDDY BEAR**
>
> A small brown teddy bear was found this morning at the Grove Nursery.
>
> He was sitting near the computer. If you are the owner, please come in and collect him.

Now I am going to re-read it all again, to make sure it makes sense. *(She then talks about the purpose of the notice.)*

I hope this notice is seen by the teddy's owner – Teddy will be so sad if he is not found by his owner

She takes the notice off the whiteboard and places it in the window of the nursery unit – the group moves with her to the window and advises on its exact position, some of the children moving outside with another practitioner in order to offer their opinion on its position.

Later that day, while the children are gathered together again, a young mother breaks into the group and says that she has read the notice and that the teddy belongs to her child. Please can she have it back? She compliments the group on the notice, saying that the large black letters really caught her eye as she walked past!

What the children have learned from this activity

This activity is a good example of a balanced approach to writing. It is rooted in a 'problem-solving' and 'thinking skills' approach to writing. Children, interested in the situation, offer solutions and the practitioner leads them towards the notion of using writing (a notice) as a way of solving the problem. She writes this non-fiction text in front of the children, talking about what she is writing and demonstrating the heading she wants to write – the children see her as a writer at work. She models the re-reading of the text – is it clear? Will this message, or notice, be understood by those who read it? Thus the underlying purpose of the writing is revealed – children have been both eavesdroppers on the writing process and an audience for the writing as it appears before them. They understand the purpose of the notice and can talk about why it was set out in a particular way – all at the tender age of four or five.

The following snapshots are all based on the same approach.

Snapshot 2 Instructions for Bob the Builder

A group of children have been sorting out the materials they are going to need in order to make a shed for Bob the Builder.

The practitioner suggests that it would be a good idea to write down on a piece of card how to make the shed so that some other children could make one as well, using these instructions.

She says the following:

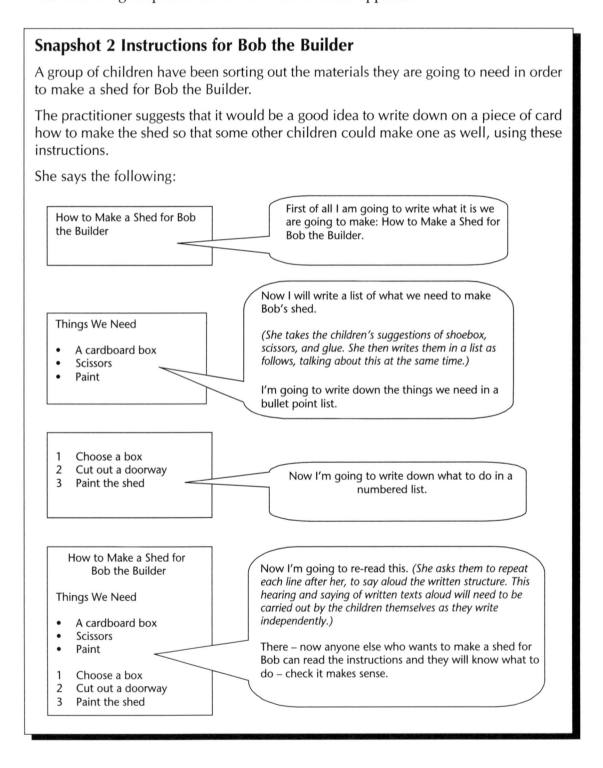

What the children have learned from this activity

Here the practitioner is demonstrating that it is useful to write. The children are learning that instructions are laid out differently from the notice in the previous snapshot and the postcard in the next snapshot.

Snapshot 3 Postcards Year R

The outdoor play area: visit to the seaside

The outdoor play area is set up as a seaside with a beach (a largish sandpit), a pool (a paddling pool complete with plastic starfish and crabs) and a seaside shop selling buckets, spades and fishing nets (complete with a shopkeeper – a practitioner in role).

A large board shows pictures and prices of the items for sale.

This was all set up following discussion with the practitioner and a group of children. Evidence of this is displayed on the wall with 'instant' or digital photographs showing the area before, during and after the 'seaside' had been created.

Children are visiting the seaside in small groups of two and three, gathered together by a practitioner, who takes them outside.

The 'shopkeeper' (another practitioner) invites them to choose an item from the board. They pay for this with some money which they have already been given because it is their turn to visit the seaside.

The children spend some time at the 'seaside' and the practitioner suggests that they 'write' a postcard and post it in the postbox.

The indoor writing corner

This is stocked with a box of picture postcards based on digital photographs of the seaside area; a team of helpers has stuck these on to the postcards. Above the table is a display of ready written, much larger postcards, which children can model their own writing on. These children have written postcards before and are familiar with the layout. At the side of the table is a postbox.

Two children take a postcard each and 'write' about their visit to the seaside; one boy takes a laminated alphabet mat (these are stored in an upright box file, always available for the children to use if they wish to).

a	b	c	d
e	f	g	h
i	j	k	l
m	n	o	p
q	r	s	t
u	v	w	x
y	z		

An alphabet mat

With great concentration, tongue between his lips, he writes his message, saying it at the same time:

> Dr Mum
> V seesd was gtl cot a cab
> Luv
> Jon
> xxx

[Dear Mum
The seaside was good. I caught a crab.
Love
Jon
xxx]

Jon has good initial letter knowledge and some visual memory of words: Mum, was, I, a and Jon. He is hearing and can write letter sounds at the beginning and end of the word; vowels or approximations of vowel sounds are in evidence. He uses the letter board to check some of the letter shapes. He is willing to have a go, independently.

His friend Dominic writes a postcard as a string of letters, some of which are in his name. As he writes, he says aloud what he is writing. The finished form looks like a postcard and for Dominic, it is just that – his personal message in a code which he can 'read', his special writing.

It translates as:

> Dear Mum,
> I made a sandcastle.
> Love
> Dominic
> x

He signs it off with a D and a wavy line – he's exhausted!

Both children post their cards in the postbox at the side of the table – they are later collected by the class 'postman' (a practitioner) and given out to children to give to the parent who collects them.

The ability of these children to write a postcard was based on their having done this many times before with an adult, who said aloud what they were going to write. This is crucial for when children come to do it by themselves.

Ongoing assessment

'Fly on the wall'

A practitioner quietly observes the children writing. She does this from a spot where she can see whether they have mastered the directionality of writing, left to right, top to bottom. She observes their strategies, e.g. using the card or not, saying aloud what it is they are going to write. She ticks her checklist if they can, rather than if they cannot. This is assessment by omission and is far more efficient.

Sitting with children in a small group

Practitioners must make time to sit with children as they write, helping them to marshal their thoughts, think aloud and say it as they write. This should happen at this emergent stage as well as other stages through Key Stages 1 and 2. It is useful if children are grouped according to ability based on an assessment of their independent attempts.

Talking to young children about their writing

> - Offer praise for the writing, e.g. *'Your writing looks interesting – well done!'*
> - Encourage the child to read it to you, e.g. *'Tell me what your special writing says, please.'*
> - Respond to the meaning first, e.g. *'I liked it when you wrote he was a big big giant – I felt really scared!'* or *'Your Mum will really like your postcard about you catching the crab!'*
> - Suggest you write it as book writing, on occasion (useful for the parent and assessment purposes), e.g. *Is it okay for me to write your message in book writing? Under your writing?*
> - Make appropriate comments which will inform and guide them about the secretarial skills you want to see, but in an informal way, e.g.
>   *'I liked the way you wrote all the letters in a straight line – just like book writing'.*
>   *'I liked the way you wrote in lines of writing, just like in books.'*
>   *'I liked the way you put spaces between your words – just like book writing.'*
>   *'I liked the way you tried out some of the sounds at the beginning of some of the words.'*
>   *'I liked the way you are trying out words – you have the beginning and end sounds in this word.'*
>   *'Well done! You have remembered how to spell Mum, was, I, a, Jon ...'*
> - Be aware of the needs of the more able child, who can respond to further challenge if requested, e.g. *'I liked what you wrote about the giant chasing Jack – can you write another sentence about how he felt when Jack ...?'*

Giving them praise

The laying of firm foundations for young writers, as illustrated above, is important. Even writers as young as three and four years old can become switched off and disenchanted by the act of writing if there is little supportive feedback. Feedback like that offered in the examples above needs to be planned and through it practitioners learn a lot about young writers. The whole aim of the Foundation Stage is that early on our future writers know that writing is to communicate meaning, that it has a real purpose and that it can be fun. The approach illustrated in the snapshots, balanced with an effective phonics and handwriting programme, as described below, will support our youngest writers.

Independent writing

Provide a well resourced, inviting area. Ensure someone is responsible for making a regular maintenance check on the supplies and arrangement of the resources because this is a high-status part of the classroom. Provide the following:

- blank forms, cards, envelopes, postcards, notelets, four-page 'story books', 'Post-its', small whiteboards and 'Magic Writing' boards;

- computer with keyboard and text to copy;
- 'inviting' writing area with text types they might wish to write displayed on the wall or in a photo album (postcards, thank-you notes, congratulations cards, etc.);
- a postbox;
- a notice board;
- files and 'in-trays' to put writing in.

Moving towards book writing: the importance of transcription skills

Children's experimental writing, using a 'personal code' to communicate, will gradually be replaced by letters which begin to match some of the sounds of the words they are saying aloud and attempting to write. Their acquisition of phonics should take place in the following order of progression, as outlined in the **'stepping stones'** progression chart in *Curriculum Guidance for the Foundation Stage*:

- the early enjoyment of rhyme at three years;
- more focused awareness of rhyme and alliteration at around four;
- the ability to hear a rhyming 'string' (whale, snail, tale);
- recognising individual letter sounds, which may start with the initial letter of their name;
- attempts at representing words by some of their letter sounds.

Of course, some children move at great speed through these stages, apparently omitting some of them; others may stick at a particular stage.

There are a number of schemes which are particularly effective in supporting the early acquisition of sounds or 'phonemes' for early reading and writing skills: Jolly Phonics, pioneered by the Jolly Learning Company, and the DfES's own scheme, Progression in Phonics. The aim is for early acquisition of the sound symbol system so that children can apply this knowledge to reading and writing contexts they enjoy, and can make sense of.

As children's phonemic knowledge develops, the practitioner can show them, in an active way, how sounds can be used to make meaning as written words.

Page 61 of the foundation guidance emphasises the need for practitioners to 'Model writing so that children can see spelling in action and recognise how to put their knowledge of sounds to full use. Encourage children to apply their own knowledge of sounds to what they write.'

Handwriting

Children also need to be able to form the letters to match the sounds; many schools are moving towards a fully joined up script from Year R.

Handwriting is a necessary and highly technical skill to be developed in a series of stepping stones from gross to fine motor skills, as outlined on pages 66 and 67 of the foundation guidance.

Watching and teaching handwriting

As children move towards the early learning goal of being able to **'use a pencil and hold it effectively to form recognisable letters, most of which are correctly formed'** (*Curriculum Guidance for the Foundation Stage*), great emphasis should be placed on small group teaching and observation of how children are holding their pencils and forming their letters. Planning should show time 'set aside' for the teaching of handwriting by experienced practitioners who know what they are doing – handwriting is truly 'taught, not caught'. There is an important lead-up to handwriting reflected in the first three bullet points below, before children move on to using a pencil.

Tools of the trade: activities and resources which support the 'stepping stones' approach to handwriting

- Games and activities to support gross motor control: large body movements, different shapes, moving in different directions.
- Activities to support fine motor control: cutting, sticking, matching, sorting, threading, drawing, repeating patterns in sand/in paint/on paper.
- Directed and free play using dough and plasticine, clay, sponges, sticks, large paintbrushes, rollers, chalk.
- Variety of pencils: colours, softnesses, thick/medium/thin, available, accessible, ready to use.
- Variety of pens: colours, thick/medium/thin, available, accessible, ready to use.
- Variety of papers: colours, thick/medium/thin, sizes, available, accessible, ready to use.

Four- and five-year-old writers in the reception class towards the end of the first year

As children move through the foundation stage they will begin to attempt longer structures than lists, labels, captions, postcards, invitations etc. The easiest 'extended' forms of writing for young children are, first, the recount linked to personal experience and, second, the writing again of a story, one they have heard many times and may even know off by heart.

The recount

Oral rehearsal

A recount:

- retells events in the order in which they happen;
- is in the past tense;
- has a focus on who was involved and what happened;
- has a scene setting opening;
- uses time connectives to show the passing of time, e.g. then, next, after.

Most children around the age of four can recount orally something which has happened to them in real life, e.g. a visit to Tesco:

'In the afternoon me and my gran went to Tesco's. She did some shopping and buyed me a comic. After we went home and had tea. Then my Mum came.'

Shared writing

Shared writing with the teacher as scribe allows the whole class to see a recount being written in front of them.

Many early years settings and Year R classrooms have adopted the idea of having a class toy which goes home with the children. Snapshot 4 provides an example of this technique in practice. Recounts produced as a result of this are immediate, interesting and engaging for children. Parents enjoy being involved and the results can be shared through the production of a class big book: *Our Travelling Teddy*.

The concept of the sentence

Although the teacher is not talking about past tense and chronological ordering of the recount, none the less these are the structures which are being demonstrated. Oral retelling of real events comes easily to most children and their oral competency in this form allows success early on. The recount is only one of the texts which they write.

Snapshot 4 A travelling bear

We join Year R with Liam sitting on the chair with the class teddy bear on his lap. The teacher has the next page of the class-made big book open, ready to write what Liam will say. She starts by saying:

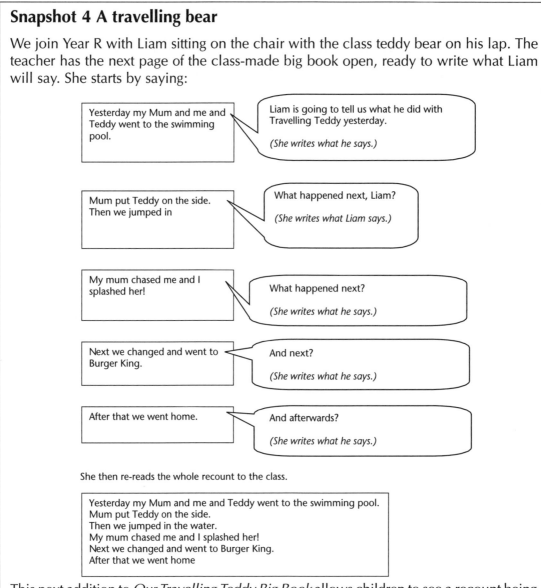

She then re-reads the whole recount to the class.

Yesterday my Mum and me and Teddy went to the swimming pool.
Mum put Teddy on the side.
Then we jumped in the water.
My mum chased me and I splashed her!
Next we changed and went to Burger King.
After that we went home

This next addition to *Our Travelling Teddy Big Book* allows children to see a recount being written from what they are saying – the links between the spoken and written language. This approach offers material for shared writing of a recount based on real experience, which for young children is an important demonstration of the immediacy of writing.

Links with reading

Our Travelling Teddy has become an important part of the reading diet in school, and is even borrowed as a 'Home Reader' which demonstrates its popularity as a writing form.

The texts that have been written are an up-to-date snapshot of children's real lives at home. There are great opportunities to develop children's cultural awareness too, e.g. recounts of a visit by Teddy to a Hindu festival, an Eid party or a wedding. These are more immediate and remembered than reading scheme or published materials.

ICT links

Travelling Teddy may be filmed on his visit or photographed using an instant or digital camera, all of which encourages interest and talk to consolidate the genre and give it a real purpose for writing.

Oral rehearsal of writing: one-to-one and small group preparation for writing in the early years

Children will need a lot of encouragement and prompting to tell a recount, in a one-to-one situation, as well as in a small group. It is well worth spending time with hesitant and unsure children. This will build up their confidence to talk and tell when they have someone who is interested in listening to them.

The practitioner needs to **model the recount** before some pupils can do it independently. This is of crucial importance for children who are learning English as an additional language, as well as for less prepared children who have English as their mother tongue.

Oral before written is a message promoted by the DfES in *Developing Early Writing (2001)*, a book on early writing at Key Stage 1, emphasising again the importance of speaking and listening skills. Time for **oral rehearsal** of the sentence is of key importance.

When working one-to-one or in a small group, begin by asking key questions that will support the writing of the recount. For example:

- Where did you go?
- When?
- Who went?
- What happened?
- What did you do at the end (of the event)?

Write the answers on your own whiteboard and display them for the children to see. Ask the children to repeat what you have written, to say it aloud – they will 'hear' the echo of these sentences when they come to write their own. Place on the wall, at eye-level, examples of the recounts which have been written, as reminders for the children.

As the children build up their confidence, run the group with the same questions, but this time expect them to write the answers. Have the alphabet mat to hand and a set of key words where they can see them, and be prepared to write in any words which they are really stuck on. The aim is to support and encourage rather than make them more anxious by withdrawing all support.

Children who find writing very difficult in these early stages need a mixed diet of telling, repeating, watching while the practitioner writes or types it for them on some occasions and having a go themselves on other occasions (still with the practitioner's encouragement). Missing out this support reinforces failure and misunderstanding, and creates switched off writers who have little or no interest in writing.

Recounts and stories

Working on recounts **first** supports the teaching of story structure, which also has a beginning–middle–end structure, like a recount. Stories are also generally written in the past tense with a complication of some kind, which allows a story to take a different direction. Something goes wrong that creates a problem and moves the focus away from what the characters are doing, as in the recount, to how they will react in the new situation that has been created (how can it be sorted out and resolved?).

Oral retelling of stories: teaching children how to write stories through story telling, storysacks and drama

Children love listening to stories, and, with some prompting, telling stories. The ability to retell a story secures story structure in readiness for when the child will write a story. Telling stories instead of reading them is a most powerful experience for children and adults, allowing them to enter into the story. These have great impact on children and are likely to be remembered in vivid detail.

Tell stories. Take the children into the story with you; watch their faces as you bring to life the characters in your head. Create pictures in their heads by the way you describe what you can see in your own imagination. To make this an easy task, use a fairy tale as the basis for your story, or learn a story off by heart. Tell a local version of a fairy tale by setting it in the local community, as in 'The gingerbread man', below.

Telling stories over and over ensures that children learn them – the story and sequence of events is already in their heads before they write.

Snapshot 5 The gingerbread man

All the children are sitting in front of the teacher ready for their story. Today the teacher is telling, rather than reading.

Mr Jones, our local baker, was making lots of gingerbread men. The children from Silverstreet Infant School loved them – their Mums often stopped to buy one on their way home. He had already baked ten trays of gingerbread men and he was feeling very tired. Hmm – he just fancied eating a warm gingerbread man with a piping hot cup of coffee.

He busied himself making a cup of coffee, saying aloud which one he would eat:

'I'll eat the one on the end with the extra big cherry for his nose.'

Mr Jones turned to put two spoonfuls of sugar in his coffee. As he did, he noticed something small and brown disappearing through the open door of the bakery – he jumped up only to see the gingerbread man he was going to eat disappearing along the street.

'Stop, stop!' he cried. 'I want to eat you!'

The gingerbread man turned and smiled and shouted: 'Run, run, as fast as you can! You can't catch me. I'm the gingerbread man!'

This story is well known to the children, but not set in their town. Their interest is caught as the gingerbread man runs through their town and into some of their gardens, meeting up with a hungry cat, dog, hamster, rabbit – and the local fox!

This version will be easy for the children to retell. They know it anyway, and children who own the animals which want to eat the gingerbread man can retell those parts of the story with some interest and conviction.

Storysacks

A storysack is a bag containing the story book, objects mentioned in the story, a scene setting picture and other things. This idea, developed by Neil Griffiths, has proved enormously popular across the country.

Make or buy storysacks. Bring the story to life with objects contained in it, which you take out of the sack as the story unfolds. Using real objects makes it easier for children to retell the sequence of a story, in readiness for when they are writing their versions of the same story. Enable the children to retell the story using the same objects by allowing them access to the sacks in small groups with another adult; this will be doubly effective if parents are allowed to take them home so that they can use them with their children.

Snapshot 6 The three billy goats gruff

We join a small group of children who have been selected for a repeat experience and telling of 'The three billy goats gruff'. This is a group of children who did not know the story at all and who found it very difficult to recall what happened in the story the first time around – a less prepared group.

They are sitting around the edge of a round cloth which has a large expanse of green synthetic grass stuck on one side, representing a lush meadow. A winding blue river made from blue glitter glue separates the grass from a rather dull patch of land made from brown felt. A wooden bridge sits over the river with a troll (a 'monster' toy) sitting under it.

Two goats, a small and a medium-size goat, are standing on the brown area of land. The adult takes out of the bag a third large goat, who joins the others. She asks the children to guess what the troll will say and they enthusiastically shout a chorus of 'Who's that trip tap tapping over my bridge?' The adult growls a reply that it is the third billy goat gruff, and the story continues . . .

The children are totally engaged in the story, lapping it up.

When the story ends they ask for it again, but this time the adult asks the children to tell the story with the aid of the toys, which they do, without hesitation.

Later they are given a set of cards which tell the story in pictures; they put these in the right order, discussing this as a group with an adult overseeing them.

The adult asks for a caption for each picture and writes these on to a set of blank cards as different children tell them to her – these are shared with the whole class on another occasion.

Next week they have the opportunity to retell the story using the sack, with a teaching assistant observing them and helping, if necessary.

Drama: acting out the stories

Drama offers the children the chance truly to enter into the story – into another time, another place, another experience. We have already seen how effective role-play can be in Snapshot 1; this is just one aspect of drama which feeds good practice. Another drama technique is to organise with the children a series of freeze frames to represent different parts of the story. These are when children use their bodies to make little frozen moments in time, from a story of poem, like a pause frame on a video film. These will be run as a sequence, following the story line. The children will be helped to sort themselves out into groups, and first to try out the scenes with no talk. Then they can practise what the various characters might say.

The teacher can read 'Jack and the Beanstalk' to the children. She tells the children what they will be acting out and then asks them to get into their groups and 'freeze'. She calls 'action' to one group at a time. In turn , each group performs for the other groups. The children are given the following scenes:

1 Jack's mother saying how poor she is.
2 Jack's mother telling him to get out of bed and sell the cow.
3 Jack on the way to market with the cow.
4 Jack, the cow and the man with the magic beans.
5 Jack and his mother see the beanstalk.

Different children perform each of the scenes.

The children are learning the following:

• that stories can be brought to life;
• that they can be acted out in the same sequence;
• that characters talk to each other, and can feel happy, sad, alone or angry.

Modelling stories as the next step: teacher demonstration

Snapshot 7 Mouse babies

Owl Babies has already been heard a number of times by the class. The teacher tells them that she is going to write another story in front of them, and that it is going to be called 'Mouse babies'.

She writes the title at the top of the page and then the first line of the story, using *Owl Babies*, by Martin Waddel, as the model.

As she writes she says the words aloud and re-reads the line when she has finished.

> **MOUSE BABIES**
>
> Once there were three baby mice: Ebony and Imran and Jo.

> They lived in a nest with their Mouse Mother.

> Now I know that mice live in nests. I'll write the next line:
>
> They lived in a nest with their Mouse Mother.

> One night they woke up and their Mouse Mother was GONE.

> Do you remember what happens next?
>
> *(The teacher listens and one child says that their mother had gone. The teacher writes the next line.)*

Using the book as a model, she then asks for contributions from the children, and scribes what they say. This session is followed up by children independently writing the end of the story, writing with a teaching assistant or the teacher in a small group, or writing one-to-one.

Chapter 3

Writing opportunities in Year 1

In this chapter we cover: performance poetry; captions; assessment and next steps; one-to-one feedback. We do this through a series of 'snapshots' in the Year 1 classroom. Children enter this year with a variety of experiences and abilities in writing.

Formative assessment is always important and Year 1 is crucial for assessing writing, given that children will have had between one and three terms in Year R.

Summer-born children, especially boys, may trail somewhat in relation to the autumn born children.

Seeking out a stimulating purpose

After half-term the teacher is taking the class to the British Museum's Africa Exhibition. This is part of the geography scheme of work, where the children have to study a contrasting locality to their own, and will result in a presentation for parents. The poems the children are going to write are to be performed, accompanied by music, dance and masks, which link to the notion of a masquerade, which is an important focus of the exhibition.

Plotting the path through the planning

Y1T2TL 13: to substitute and extend patterns from reading, e.g. adding further rhyming words, lines.
KS1EN1 (speaking and listening) 3: group discussion and interaction.
KS1EN1 4a: to use language and actions to explore and convey characters and emotions.
KS1GEO 6: study of a locality overseas.
KS1 ART & DESIGN 4b: materials and processes used in making art, craft and design.
KS1 MUSIC 4d: how music is used for particular purposes.

The teacher capitalises on children's prior knowledge of John Agard's poem (see below), which is to be the basis for the writing.

Snapshot 1 Performance poetry

We join the class as they are giving a performance of John Agard's 'Don't call alligator long-mouth till you cross river'. They do this with great vigour and much enjoyment.

In place is a large TV monitor, attached to the computer, which is useful for demonstrating writing. The teacher displays the poem on screen, as below.

Don't call alligator long-mouth till you cross river

Call alligator long-mouth
call alligator saw-mouth
call alligator pushy-mouth
call alligator scissors-mouth
call alligator raggedy-mouth
call alligator bumpy-bum
call alligator all dem rude word
but better wait
    till you cross river.

Talking through what you want to teach

The teacher explains that she is going to change some of the words and make a new poem. This is going to be part of their presentation to parents and they will all learn it off by heart. She wants to change it into an African poem. These poems will be performed as part of their Africa concert for parents at the end of term.

Showing how to do it

The children listen in on the teacher's thoughts:

'I want to make this poem into an African one by choosing the name of a scary African animal – I'll highlight alligator and replace it with crocodile.'

The following changes appear on screen:

Don't call alligator long-mouth
    till you cross river

Don't call crocodile long-mouth
    till you cross river

    Call crocodile long-mouth
    call crocodile saw-mouth
    call crocodile pushy-mouth
    call crocodile scissors-mouth
    call crocodile raggedy-mouth
    call crocodile bumpy-bum
    call crocodile all dem rude word
    but better wait
        till you cross river.

Two are printed off: one for the classroom wall and one for their 'Africa' big book.

The children are asked if they know of any other African animals that are scary, just like the crocodile in the new poem.

They come up with the following list, with some help from the teacher, including some toy animals and pictures: lion, tiger, leopard, panther, elephant, snake.

Various animals are handed out to writing groups and children are asked to brainstorm five words they can think of to describe the mouths of these animals – on their small whiteboards, in pairs. They are asked to attach these words with a dash, followed by the word 'mouth', exactly as John Agard had done. To support them further the teacher shows them exactly what she wants:

> 'I'm going to write one for you. I think this lion has a roaring mouth, so I am going to write it like this.'

> roaring-mouth

They are given ten minutes to do this. The crocodile poem is kept on screen. The children return after ten minutes and sit in a circle. Each pair is asked to name their animal and share their words.

Lucy and Aziz come up with the following list, which will be used by the teacher in tomorrow's poem: 'big-mouth, scary-mouth, roaring-mouth, dribbling-mouth, horrible-mouth'.

Snapshot 2 Day 2

We join the session with John Agard's poem on screen. Now it is the children's turn to make suggestions to the teacher. They choose to replace 'alligator' with 'lion':

Showing them how to do it

The teacher talks them through it, asking where they want her to put the new words.

This is a lion poem, so I'll highlight alligator and replace it with lion. Now I'll read it aloud.

Don't call lion long-mouth
   till you cross river

Lucy and Aziz, tell me your new word to replace 'long-mouth'. 'Big-mouth', I like that, I've seen a lion yawn and he does indeed have a big mouth!

Don't call lion big-mouth
   till you cross river

Now we have a problem – lions don't live in rivers. Does anyone know where a lion lives? Yes, a plain – rather like a huge field with no fences.

Lucy and Aziz, is it all right if I change the word river to plain? Okay – there is our title:

Don't call lion big-mouth till you cross plain

The children go on to contribute their words and the finished poem is:

Don't call lion big-mouth till you cross plain

Call lion big-mouth
Call lion scary-mouth
Call lion horrible-mouth
Call lion sharp-mouth
Call lion roaring-mouth
call lion all dem rude word
but better wait
    till you cross plain

By Lucy and Aziz

How this activity has helped Year 1 writers

This poem is an ideal choice as a scaffold for writing a new one. By merely changing the noun 'alligator' we have a new poem. With minimal change, e.g. the lion poem, a new poem has been created.

Without too much hard work, then, children can experience the satisfaction of writing a new version. This is great for self-esteem and a positive attitude towards writing.The teacher facilitated the process by demonstrating how to write a version using their ideas. It can be summed up as:

Read (the model)

Watch the teacher demonstrate how to write one like it

Say (rehearse the words)

Write one like it

Guided writing with struggling writers

The lowest achieving group sit around the computer and rehear a poem about a tiger. The teacher types in the words and each child receives a printed copy to take home.

Call tiger huge-mouth
Call tiger dribbling-mouth
Call tiger nasty-mouth
Call tiger stripey-mouth
Call tiger yellow-mouth
call tiger all dem rude word
but better wait
    till you cross jungle

The class teacher and a well briefed teaching assistant join the other groups throughout the week, at different stages of the writing.

All groups manage to type the poems on screen and print them off by the end of the week, some helped by the teaching assistant.

All the poems are stuck into a big book. A parallel class choose several of the new versions, learn them and perform them for the class. This gives the children an audience for their writing, with the accompanying reward of seeing and hearing their new poems performed in public. These will all be used in their African concert for the parents.

Writing captions in Year 1: how are our toys different from those in the past?

Seeking out a stimulating purpose

The Year 1 teacher had invested a lot of time in the children handling, talking about, sorting and describing a collection of toys from the 1950s to the present day. She had used the QCA unit for Year 1 pupils (taken from the QCA schemes of work) as the planning for this work in history. She had taken 'instant' or digital photographs of each toy.

The photographs and writing were going to be displayed in the corridor in a time-line order from the 1950s to the present day. Parents would become an audience for this writing in a more active way than usual, by jotting down comments about the display on 'Post-it' notes. The children could read these and give feedback to the teachers on what parents thought.

Plotting the path through the planning

> Y1T3 21: to use the language and features of non-fiction texts, e.g. captions and labels.
> KS1ENG 1: speaking and listening – all of 1 and 2, speaking and listening.
> KS1HISTORY 1a: place objects in chronological order.

Year 1 writers need very careful handling. Many will have passed through the emergent stage of writing and moved into constructing meaning using the transcriptional skills they feel secure with, such as using plausibly phonetic alternatives (e.g. 'haf' for 'have', 'v' for 'the'), and forming their letters mainly as they have been taught to in discrete handwriting lessons. They still very much write as they speak, very often connecting streams of talk with 'and' or 'and then' to signal chronological time in a recount or a story. Use of 'and' or 'and then' connectives reflects the children's difficulty in distancing themselves from the spoken form of English as they write. Adopting a 'writerly' style is greatly supported by the teacher demonstrating what she does as she constructs a sentence. The construction of a sentence through non-fiction is much easier than that for stories.

Talking through what you want to teach

The children had the task clearly explained to them, which was to write several captions and/or labels for each photograph. The purpose of their writing was to explain to visiting parents or other children:

1 The name of the toy.
2 When it was made.
3 What it looked like.
4 What children did with it.

Showing how to do it

Snapshot 3 Writing captions

The teacher shows them a boxed set of Lego and demonstrates to the class how to write a set of captions.

I'm going to start with the first caption: the name of the toy.

This is a Lego set.

Now I'm going to write when it was made.

It was made in 1966.

Now I'm going to look inside the box and take out some Lego. I'm going to write what it looks like.

It has lots of plastic pieces.

Now you talk with your friend and practise a sentence that begins with 'Children' and says what they did with it. *(She gives the children time to talk together and then listens to several children's feedback.)*

Children fixed them together to make things. I like that and will write it.

Children fixed them together to make something.

The completed text is shown below.

> This is a Lego set.
> It was made in 1966.
> It has lots of plastic pieces.
> Children fixed them together to make something.

The rest of the hour is given over to the groups of four children writing a set of captions about a Sindy doll, using exactly the same approach, helped by this list:

1 The name of the toy.
2 When it was made.
3 What it looked like.
4 What children did with it.

Children who were struggling with this concept were given sentence frames to help them:

> This is a ....
>
> It was made in ....
>
> It has ....
>
> Children ....

The finished product looked like this:

> This is a Sindy doll.
> It was made in 1968.
> She is very thin.
> Children played with her at home.

What the children learned from this

There is a particular form of writing to go with non-fiction texts. Sentences contain information about the toys. These are easy to write because they give facts about the toy. The same format can be used over and over again. It helps your writing if you have already said it aloud to a friend. Stick to the formula of writing one fact in each sentence, and you can't go wrong.

There is a real purpose to their writing, which is to give information about something.

There is an audience for their writing because it will be read by adults and children who walk past it in the corridor. The teacher has used this idea before and noted that the children were very interested in the response from other children and adults to their writing. This should provide motivation for them to write more.

Snapshot 4 Get up and go

To focus the children's attention on the necessity for more than one piece of information about each toy, the teacher designed this 'get up and go' activity.

She had already written several sets of captions about certain toys. Every card in each set had a picture of the toy on the back. The actual toy was on display with a label attached, which showed the year it was first made. There were four captions in each set (see below).

A get up and go 'sort the captions' activity

We join the teacher as she is placing four hoops in the centre of the circle in which the children are sitting. In each hoop she places one of the following captions:

The name of the toy	When it was made
What it looked like	What children did with it

She quickly hands out all the cards to the children and asks them to read out their caption if it says the name of the toy. These children move together into the appropriate hoop with the following cards:

This is a water pistol.	This is Tiny Tears.
This is a Rubik's cube.	This is a space hopper.

The teacher then asks four children to move into the 'When it was made' hoop.

It was made in 1962.	It was made in 1975.

It was made in 1955.	It was made in 1980.

Next the children are asked to move into the 'What it looks like' hoop.

It looks like a gun.	It is a baby doll.

It is a cube with 6 different colours.	It looks like a ball with ears.

Finally, the remaining four children move into the 'What children did with it' hoop.

They filled it with water and squirted it.	They fed it and nursed it.

They twisted it until each side was the same colour.	They sat on it and bounced around.

Now the teacher asks four different children who are sitting in the circle to move the children in the hoops around until each hoop has a complete set of captions about one of the toys. The children then fetch the correct toy and place it in the correct hoop.

A different way in

It is important to offer children some variety in the way we structure a literacy hour. This 'get up and go' approach is active, interesting and a 'different way in' to emphasising the sorting of captions about one toy.

Once each set was complete the class was asked to read aloud the captions. The children then fixed each set to the whiteboard.

Assessment in action: an audit on writing

It is very important for all pupils that the class teacher conducts an audit of writing at some time in the autumn term and every half-term from then on (see the assessment activity at the end of this chapter). This is to assess what children are able to do and what their attitudes to writing are, and it is absolutely vital for small guided writing groups. It is important to give 'positive strokes' to them as young (and possibly) struggling writers. A key marker for progress is the ability to construct a sentence. This may not show correct punctuation, e.g. capital letter and full stop, but may 'read' as a series of sentences connected with 'and', e.g. I went to the park and played on the swings and had an ice cream.

The purpose of the assessment activity is to celebrate strengths and progress and take a next steps approach to whole-class issues.

The initial read through results in a crude sorting of children into a developmental progression from Level 1 to 2 National Curriculum levels. Five groups emerge:

- one group working towards Level 1;
- two groups working at Level 1;
- two groups working at Level 2c.

All the writing samples were independent attempts at writing a recount of something which had happened in the holidays.

The teacher took one sample from the middle ability of each of the five groups and assessed them using the grid in Figure 3.1. This assessment model gave the teacher feedback on the progress of her young writers and a template for action for the following half-term.

Box 1
- Gives the level and which term the assessment took place (bold and underlined)
- Asks for an attitude comment (poor, fair, positive)
- Asks for the reading level of that child, because limited reading diet can equate with limited writing. (The levels relate to those found in *Bookbands for Guided Reading*, UK Reading Recovery Network, 2000.)

Box 2
- Features of the text type: how close the child is in meeting the requirements of the genre he or she is trying out
- Content: what is written
- Sentence structure: the developmental point the child is at: understood, simple, compound, complex
- Vocabulary: showing some variety and suitability
- Punctuation: capital letter and full stop to signal boundaries of the sentence

Pupil Level:	Term: Au1, Au2, Spr1, Spr2, Sum1, Sum2
Attitude to writing:	
Reading Level:	

Features of the text type	
Content	
Sentence structure	
Vocabulary	
Punctuation	
Spelling	
Handwriting	

Figure 3.1

Using assessed examples with the whole class

Teachers can use examples of writing like those assessed below during whole-class sessions on writing by copying them on to OHTs. This approach gives children the chance to hear from the teacher and see in front of them the **strengths** of a piece of writing and **one or two** ideas for improvement. The emphasis for improvement should lie in the meaning and structure rather than on spelling and an overemphasis on capital letters and full stops.

Guided writing

Work in a group of no more than six children offers another opportunity for feedback on writing, which may be during the construction of sentences or after one or two have been completed. Oral feedback like this gives more effective 'payback' than any amount of written comments on the bottom of a child's work in isolation from the child.

One-to-one feedback: a 'golden' writing conference

Take time for a 'writing conference' twice during the year for every child in the class. This is well worth the effort and organisation from the teacher for the child to feel that the teacher is interested in him or her at a personal rather than group level. Use the 'golden-line' approach, using a special gold marker pen to show children what their strengths are as writers and to give them an achievable 'next steps' target.

Taking forward these issues: a 'next steps' approach

Group 5: the 'working towards Level 1' group

Children were still at the early stages of emergent writing and the middle ability child in the example below revealed the following writing development:

I wt to see Billy bb a p c (in the park).

Pupil Level: W   Term: **Au1,** Au2, Au3, Spr1, Spr2, Spr3, Sum1, Sum2, Sum3
Attitude to writing: positive
Reading level: Book Band 2

Features of the text type; recount	Past tense – wt = went One event
Content	Writing communicates meaning
Sentence structure	Simple sentence (understood)
Vocabulary	Factual, accurate
Punctuation	None
Spelling	Some letter shapes in response to sound + random letters
Handwriting	

Next steps

Whole class:

- Teacher demonstration of writing a sentence.
- Shared writing of a sentence.
- Oral rehearsal of a sentence.
- Supported composition of a sentence.

Small group:

- Writing a sentence with a teacher assistant and a sound alphabet picture chart.
- Phoneme counting of cvc (consonant, vowel, consonant) words.
- Overlearning of high-frequency words.
- Watching and teaching handwriting.

Group 4: the 'Level 1' group

we tuk r dog to the pk and he rund awa

Pupil Level: 1   **Au1,** Au2, Au3, Spr1, Spr2, Spr3, Sum1, Sum2, Sum3 Attitude to writing: reluctant Reading Level: Book Bands 3

Features of the text type: **recount**	Written in the past tense
	Two connected events
Content	Writing communicates meaning
Sentence structure	One long sentence connected with 'and' (compound sentence)
Vocabulary	Appropriate words used in context
Punctuation	None
Spelling	We, to, the, and, he correct; dog – cvc; hearing beginning, end and middle phonemes
Handwriting	

Next steps

Whole class:

- Teacher demonstration of writing a sentence.
- Shared writing of a sentence.
- Oral rehearsal of a sentence.
- Supported composition of a sentence.
- Adding in different connectives (then, so, but).
- Phoneme counting using vowel digraph work from *Jolly Phonics* (sound buttons: segmentation of phonemes).
- Overlearning of more high-frequency words.

Small group:

- Attitude: combat reluctance to write by linking writing to real experience, e.g. parent bringing in a photo, or teaching assistant taking a photo on a digital camera, in the playground, coming into school. Writing based on this.
- Demonstration in the small group of writing a recount with more than two events, using who, what, where, why, when cards.
- Writing with a sound card at hand to identify initial and other phonemes in the word.

Group 3: the 'Level 1' group

We went to the prek and we sor a zebre and we feydid it grase then we had a iys creme and then we went home.

Pupil Level: 1   **Au1,** Au2, Au3, Spr1, Spr2, Spr3, Sum1, Sum2, Sum3
Attitude to writing: positive
Reading Level: Book Bands 4

Features of the text type	Series of events written in the past tense – who, where, what
Content	Events simple but in a logical order; interesting introduction of a zebra in the park
Sentence structure	Very long sentence connected with and, then
Vocabulary	Words are simple but appropriate
Punctuation	Capital letter at the beginning of the sentence
Spelling	11 h f words correct; plausible phonemic alternatives
Handwriting	

Next steps

Whole class:

- As above.

Small group:

- Small guided group to support the writing of all features of the recount, including why and when.
- Oral rehearsal of sentences in a circle where pupils hold up a full stop to chunk the recount into shorter sentences. Re-reading writing to check for overuse of 'and then'.

Groups 1 and 2: the Level 2c groups

On holiday we went to EuroDisney with are mum and we lived in EuroDisney. My mum was called Susannah and my sister was calle Natasha we went on a trip and we went to the park then we saw the dolfins. they was jumping reely hiy and they jumped rite through the hoops and we were splashed by water but we liked it. Then we all had a Big Mac and then we went to the hotel. It was fun.

Pupil Level: 2c **Au1**, Au2, Au3, Spr1, Spr2, Spr3, Sum1, Sum2, Sum3
Attitude to writing: good
Reading Level: Book Bands 5

Features of the text type	Series of events in the past tense – who, what, when, why, where
Content	Informative list of things they did on holiday with a last sentence which reflects on their enjoyment
Sentence structure	Mostly simple sentences connected with 'and' and 'then'; one compound sentence at the end connected with 'but'
Vocabulary	Some lively phrases, e.g. 'jumping reely hiy' and 'rite through the hoops'
Punctuation	Correct capital letters at the beginning of four sentences and for names. Four full stops used correctly.
Spelling	Most hf words spelled correctly; plausible phonemic alternatives
Handwriting	

Next steps

Whole class:

• As above.

Small group:

• Small guided group to support the writing of all features of the recount.
• Oral rehearsal of sentences in a circle where pupils hold up a full stop to chunk the recount into shorter sentences.
• Demonstration of how to re-read writing to check for overuse of 'and then'.
• Oral rehearsal of sentences with focus on correct use of 'was' and 'were'.
• Encouragement to add 'but' in a sentence.

Chapter 4

Moving on in Year 2

In this chapter we cover: more able writers; story beginnings; planning; struggling writers; local study reports.

Writers at this stage really start to lift off and can become increasingly confident independent writers. We look at how we can use our assessment to teach children at their point of need in a stimulating and exciting way.

More able writers in Year 2: a guided writing experience

Snapshot 1 Using what they read to improve how they write

The children have a small photograph album in front of them. This contains a selection of beginnings from published children's stories and they are discussing with their friends which beginning will suit their story. Their discussion is related to simple filled in story plans in front of them which were based on the story of Red Riding Hood (see the blank version below).

Planning My Story

Who?	Where?	When?

Problem?

Which beginning?

Which ending?

They have mastered story structure and the notion of a problem or conflict of some kind to propel the story along. The teacher has worked with them in a small group with the objective of improving their writing style in the ways in which they open and close their stories. She decided to use real authors' writing to help them and the photo album has samples of beginnings and endings of stories, on which they can model their own. Each extract is described in 'child-friendly' language at the side. Three beginnings are shown below.

Story beginnings

Begin by one character telling the other main character what to do	'Little Bean, stop messing around and get ready! We're going on holiday!'

From John Wallace, *Little Bean's Holiday* (Collins Picture Lions).

Begin by describing something the character liked doing	Thulani loved to bask all day in the sun.

From Dianne Stewart, *The Gift of the Sun* (Frances Lincoln).

Begin by describing three good things about the main character	Badger was dependable, reliable, and always ready to lend a helping paw.

From Susan Varley, *Badger's Parting Gifts* (Collins Picture Lions).

Plotting a path through planning for the more able

The teacher's planning showed differentiation for three groups: average, underattaining and **more able**. The children in this more able group were excellent readers and their writing was imaginative, lively and peppered with interesting vocabulary from their reading. The teacher's aim was to see if the 'modelling' approach as suggested in the National Literacy Strategy could be used to improve the literary qualities of their openings and endings. The above extracts were all taken from books the children had read. They had already been given the task in a small independent group reading session of identifying the ways in which these writers started off and/or ended their stories.

> The objectives for this work were taken from Y3T1TL 12: 'to investigate and collect sentences for story openings and endings – use some of these formal elements in re-telling and story writing'.

Snapshot 1 continued

Talking through what it is you want to teach

The teacher starts with the oral rehearsal of some of these sentence structures linked to characters in Red Riding Hood.

The following teacher talk takes place during a guided writing session.

Now write down three good things you can think about (Red Riding Hood). Just write words – don't worry about writing sentences.

Let's share together what you have: kind, caring, thoughtful, helpful, happy. Well done – these words will be useful for later.

Now write down bad things you can think about the wolf. Okay, let's share what it is you have written. 'Bad, cruel, wicked, greedy, horrible, cunning, sly' – well, you have thought of more bad words than good words!

Now – this is the challenge I have for you. I want you to start off your stories by describing one of these characters. However, you have to write a sentence modelled on this one from *Badger's Parting Gifts*:

Badger was dependable, reliable, and always ready to lend a helping paw

The author (Susan Varley) tells us three facts about Badger:

He was dependable.
He was reliable.
He was helpful.

Okay – now choose three words from your list and say a sentence like the one about Badger.

The children contribute the following sentences on their whiteboards:

'The Wolf was sly, cunning, and always hungry.'

'The Wolf was wicked, greedy, and always ready to trick someone.'

'Red Riding Hood was kind, happy, and always pleased to visit her Granny.'

'Red Riding Hood was caring, kind, and always ready to help someone.'

Okay – now write them down.

The teacher moves around the group, checking and advising at the point of writing. The children then use one of their sentences to start off their story.

As they near the end of their story the teacher expects them to choose one of the ways of ending their story drawn from the endings in the small photo album.

What the children learned from this activity

They were learning to use more literary structures than they were accustomed to.

The National Literacy Strategy objective 'to investigate beginnings and endings' is key to this – all these books had been read by the children but none of them had ever used a construction like this one in their writing. Carry over of vocabulary seemed to be happening in their writing, but there was no carry over of complex sentences like these.

There is a place for a focus on reading a book with the 'eye of a writer' as part of the reading experience for fluent readers at Key Stage 1.

Children are naturally keen to take the message of the book without noticing much about style, but it is an area which can be very usefully explored with able readers at Key Stage 1, as well as at Key Stage 2. With regular experience of this as part of the reading diet, the expectation is that it will have more of an impact on their writing. But it will need the support of the teacher during guided writing sessions, as described above.

Switching young writers on in Year 2

Seeking out a stimulating purpose

A lot of work has been covered with a struggling group of writers in Year 2. Many of them are boys. Their handwriting and spelling skills show great improvement but they still show a lack of interest in writing, especially in story writing. What can the teacher do to motivate them? She decides to use some drama approaches to see if this spotlight can switch them on. She does this with the whole class.

Plotting a path through the planning

The teacher decided to approach the writing through using a toy to catch their interest. She chose to focus on one key objective:

> Y2T1TL1 1: to use language of time to structure a series of events, e.g. 'when I had finished...', 'suddenly...', 'after that'.

Showing how to do it

Snapshot 2 A character in search of a story

When the children come into the classroom, the chairs have been arranged in a circle. In the middle of the circle is a small table and on the table a shiny golden box. A caption is in front of the box. It says:

> **A character in search of a story**

The teacher asks the class what she should do – what could be in the box?

They beg her to open it and she does – very gingerly!

You could hear a pin drop in the class. She brings out a rather bedraggled teddy bear with a forlorn expression.

She keeps the children's interest by thinking aloud about his plight.

> I wonder who he is. He looks really sad. Oh, he's really dirty – I wonder what could have happened to him.

The children, including the boys, can't wait to contribute ideas. Empathy with the bear's situation is a powerful tool to pull children into narrative thinking. The teacher narrows the options down to the bear being left outside during some bad weather, perhaps a storm of some kind.

Demonstration writing

Timmy fell to the ground but nobody noticed. They packed their picnic away and disappeared through the trees.

> I'm going to start the story.
>
> I'm going to call the teddy Timmy. I agree with you – he does look frightened. I'm going to start my story by Timmy being dropped outside, like the teddy in Home Before Dark which I read to you last week. He was dropped in a park – I'm going to drop Timmy in a dark, dark wood!

He could see some dark shapes.

> Turn to your friend – think about what Timmy could see.
>
> Tell me one of your sentences – 'He could see some dark shapes'. I like that – I'll write it down.

Timmy fell to the ground but nobody noticed. They packed their picnic away and disappeared through the trees.

He could see some dark shapes.

The next thing he saw was . . .

> L*et's read what we have written*

> F*inish off this sentence on your whiteboards....*

The teacher reads what the children have written, comments on what they have done well and offers ideas for improvement.

> Now I want you to finish off this story – remember to use some of these words at the beginning of several of your sentences to show that time was moving along
>
> Then . . . Next . . . Finally . . .

The children are then all given the opportunity to complete the story, which they do without any hesitation. The teacher emphasises how important it is to stop at intervals as they write to reread and check for meaning.

What the children have learned

They have learned that writing can be an enjoyable experience when you are interested in how a character is going to find his way out of a tricky situation. They have also learned that the children themselves must solve this situation to resolve it in some way – as active authors at work.

The use of a simple device like a toy can be very effective in engaging children in the act of writing. The situation conjured up by the children in partnership with the teacher leads to a compelling desire to write for a real purpose – to sort out the bear's problems.

Finding the balance

This approach to writing is not new. However, the skill of the teacher is not only in interesting the children and creating a desire to talk and write about a character's plight, but also in showing them how to do it via the demonstration, shared and supported composition model.

A Year 2 local study report: writing non-chronological reports with a cross-curricular link with Year 2

Seeking out a stimulating purpose for writing

One of the teachers has the idea of asking the children to write a report for an information pack for any new children and their parents coming to the school. The report will be accompanied by some video material of the local area. The teachers have neither the equipment nor the expertise to produce a polished video so they have to keep it simple. They will choose five of the most important locations in the town and simply point the camera at each of them for 30 seconds. This will produce a two and a half minute video without sound. The children will write a paragraph about each of the locations. This should help them to structure their report. They will then read their report aloud to the rest of the class as the video is playing. Reading it out loud will contribute to meeting one of the speaking and listening objectives. It will be challenging, interesting and fun, as well as being of real use to the school.

Some of the children will read out their reports in assembly to the rest of the school while the video is playing. A book will be made of copies of all their writing, placed in a plastic wallet with a copy of the video and entered into the school library. No doubt, some use will be made of it on school open evening. A presentation by the children will also be made at a governors' meeting.

Plotting out the path for planning

The end of the school year is drawing near, the weather is fine and the teachers want to take advantage of the opportunities for fieldwork. They know that children will write better non-chronological reports if they have clear guidelines on how to structure the information and shape the sentences, as well as some first-hand experience to write about. The children will also learn how to write and use plans to guide their writing. The contents for a lively and interesting report lie all around them. A visit has been arranged to collect information about the local area. They are to become researchers, going on an expedition to 'mine' the information they need. There are clearly some very useful links to geography.

The objectives they will bundle together are

> Y2T3TL21: to write non-chronological reports based on structure of known texts, e.g. *there are two sorts of x...;They live in x...; the As have x...; but the Bs etc.*, using appropriate language to present, sequence and categorise ideas.
> SL1: to read text aloud with intonation and expression appropriate to grammar and punctuation.
> SL5: to write in clear sentences using capital letters and full stops accurately.
> EN1KS1 1a: to speak clearly, fluently and confidently to different people, pupils should be taught to speak with clear diction and appropriate intonation.
> EN KS1 2a: to listen, understand and respond to others, pupils should be taught to sustain concentration.
> EN KS1 10c: the range of purposes should include commenting and reporting.
> GEO 3a: identify and describe what places are like.

Teachers have been working hard throughout the year to build the children's capacity to use a variety of sentences. Children will be taught how to write complex sentences appropriate to the genre. This goes beyond the National Literacy Strategy framework. Teachers have assessed children's work carefully this year and they have set targets for children appropriate to their stage of development. Many children are ready to use a wider range of subordinating connectives (e.g. so, because, until) and have been set targets for this.

Talking through what you want to teach

The teacher has a very clear idea of the teaching points she wants to make about writing non-chronological reports. These include:

- Their purpose is to tell someone about 'the way something is', to describe something (Alton town).
- The report needs a title which tells everyone what it is about.
- Each part of the report tells you about a different aspect.
- It gives the reader facts.
- Two or more facts can be put in one sentence.
- At the end of it you know more than you did when you started reading it.

During shared reading of the text below, the teacher makes explicit the connection between reading this report and the writing the children are going to be doing later. She leads a discussion about choosing the four most important things they can learn from their shared reading that will help them in their own writing. They decide on what are the most important things to remember. She writes them up as 'Golden Rules for Writing a Report':

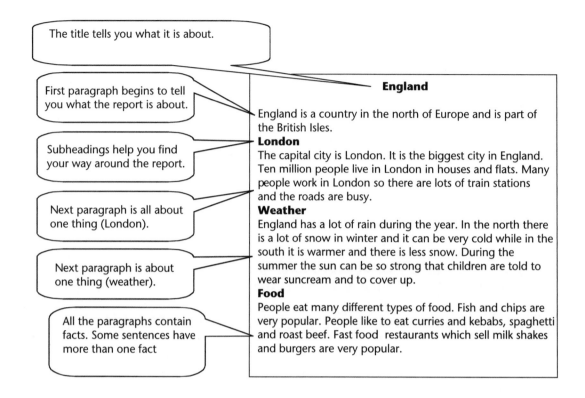

The title tells you what it is about.

First paragraph begins to tell you what the report is about.

Subheadings help you find your way around the report.

Next paragraph is all about one thing (London).

Next paragraph is about one thing (weather).

All the paragraphs contain facts. Some sentences have more than one fact

England

England is a country in the north of Europe and is part of the British Isles.

London

The capital city is London. It is the biggest city in England. Ten million people live in London in houses and flats. Many people work in London so there are lots of train stations and the roads are busy.

Weather

England has a lot of rain during the year. In the north there is a lot of snow in winter and it can be very cold while in the south it is warmer and there is less snow. During the summer the sun can be so strong that children are told to wear suncream and to cover up.

Food

People eat many different types of food. Fish and chips are very popular. People like to eat curries and kebabs, spaghetti and roast beef. Fast food restaurants which sell milk shakes and burgers are very popular.

Golden Rules for Writing a Report

- Only write facts.
- Start with an introduction.
- Write subheadings.
- Group the information into paragraphs.

The children know they are going to use this structure to write a report themselves.

Snapshot 3 Making a plan of the writing journey

They are going to write a report about the school. The teacher begins by writing a simple writing plan on the board. She tells them that she is making this plan because it will help her to think of ideas to write, and to remember them. It will be like a map, so that when she starts writing she knows what to write and where she is going. She says she will help them write their plan for their report.

The children are told that the audience for their writing is new children and their parents coming to the school. The children have to suggest what they think would interest these readers and what they would want to know about their school. She gives them some headings and asks them to jot down on their whiteboards all the things they think are important, e.g. uniforms, building, where it is. Using this information the teacher constructs this plan in front of them.

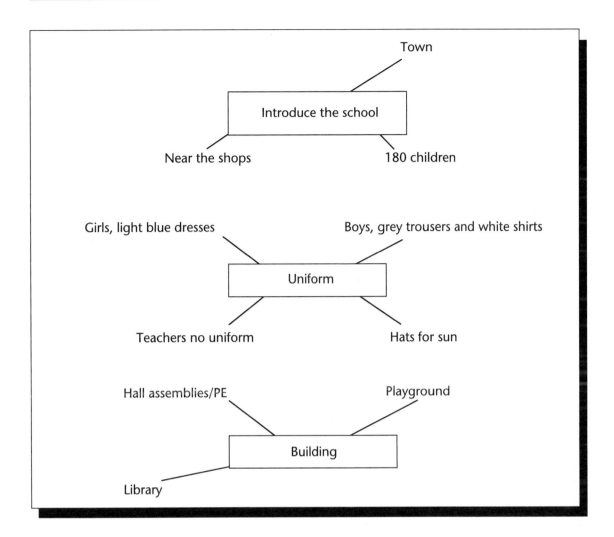

Snapshot 4 The sound of writing: showing how to write a report on the school

In shared writing, the teacher now uses the plan to demonstrate how to write a report just like the one they know they are going to write themselves later. This should give them a much better chance of getting the structure right first time.

It is vital that the teacher now overtly makes use of the plan, referring to it throughout the shared writing session. She begins to speak to the children.

Who can remember what good writers do?

Yes! They gather their ideas and then they say the sentence, see if it sounds right and then they write it and, finally, they read it back to check it says what they want it to.

Now I am going to try to remember those things as I write. You listen and watch to see if I do them.

I want this report to be for new children so I want to include things they need to know.

I need an introductory sentence. Let's see what we put on our plan to remind me.

Friary School is in Alton, near London. That sounds good. Let's write it. It introduces us very well.

> Friary School is in Alton, near London

Let's put some more detail.

It is near the shops. there are 180 children in the school.

It is near the shops. there are 180 children in the school.

Let me read it back. Whoops! I forgot the capital letter. Does anybody else do that? Yes. Some of us have that as a writing target. It's a good thing I read it back or I wouldn't have noticed.

Now for the next paragraph. We want to write all about the uniform. I'll write the subheading. If we look at our plan we can get some help. With the person beside you make up the next sentence

(Children talk with their 'carpet buddies' and then offer suggestions. The teacher listens and then decides on one to use, explaining why)

I like the sentence *'All the children wear uniform but the teachers do not'* because it is to the point and the use of the gluing word 'but' is really effective. I am going to follow it with the sentence *'Girls have to wear light blue dresses and boys wear polo shirts and grey trousers'* because new children will really need to know that.

Friary School is in Alton near London.

It is near the shops. There are 180 children in the school.

Uniform
All the children wear uniform but the teachers do not. Girls have to wear light blue dresses and boys wear polo shirts and grey trousers.

Hot weather
When it is sunny children have to wear hats to protect them.

What do I do now. Yes! Read it back. It is best not to leave it until the end but keep reading back as you write.

Now. Let's look at the plan. We had better mention about what we do when it is very hot. I'll write the subheading. Make up a sentence with your carpet buddy.

(The teacher listens and then decides on one to use, explaining why. She writes it on the board)

Let's read it back together. What do you think? *(Listens to their evaluation)*

All the information about the same thing is together. I think the plan really helped us, don't you?

Snapshot 5 Making the video

The children are taken on a walk around Alton. They collect information about the town. At some locations the teachers have arranged for them to be met by people who will tell them about that part of the town, e.g. the manager of the sports centre, a volunteer at the steam railway station and the vicar at the church. A two and a half minute video is made by pointing the school camera for 30 seconds at each of five key locations.

They must write the report to go with it. The teachers help the children to write a plan in shared writing and it is put on the wall for all to see and refer to. The more able are expected to write their own plan and they do so in a guided writing session which works more like a 'mini-shared writing', except that the teacher does not scribe – the children write their own.

Images used in the video

The High
Street

The Butts
Green

The railway
station

The children are then given time to write. Some writing is photocopied on to acetate and discussed with the whole class on the overhead projector.

When the reports are finished they read them out loud as the silent video is played, matching each paragraph against the 30-second image. Children comment on how effectively others have presented their reports. These are gathered into a book with photos of the locations. This all goes in the library with a copy of the video tape and an audio recording of them reading out loud so other children can hear it and read it in the library. The children prepare for a governors' meeting, where all of this will be presented.

Figure 4.1 shows a plan written by one of the more able children. He has decided what the main focus of each paragraph will be and he has recorded this in the bubbles. Around the bubbles he has organised information that will be of interest to the reader (or listener).

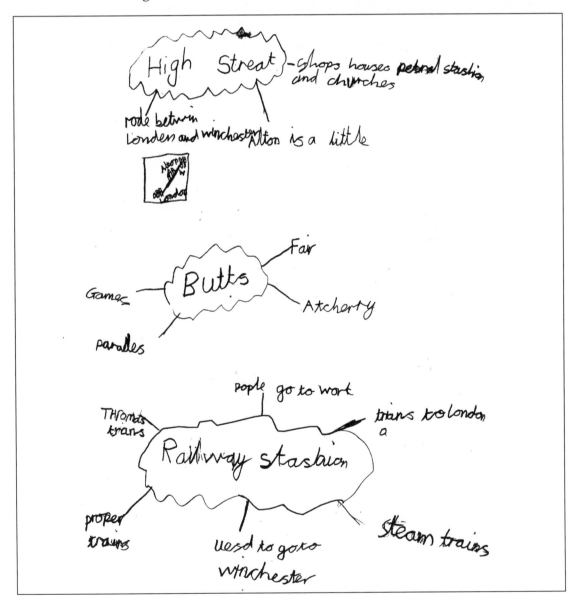

Figure 4.1

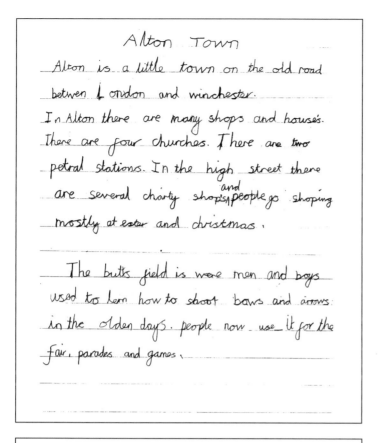

Alton Town

Alton is a little town on the old road between London and winchester.
In Alton there are many shops and houses. There are four churches. There are two petral stations. In the high street there are several charity shops and people go shopping mostly at ester and christmas.

The butts field is were men and boys used to lern how to shoot bows and arrows in the olden days. people now use it for the fair, parades and games.

The station is very important to Alton because many people go to work in london. It used to go to winchester. There are many trains, steam trains Thomas trains and proper trains. some times morris men come and dance on the second platform.

Figure 4.2

In Figure 4.2, the writer has used the golden rules of writing reports. He has recorded facts rather than personal opinions. There is an introduction to the report to orientate the reader and he has gathered information about the same aspects together in paragraphs. He has clearly referred back to his plan, which has helped him to organise his writing.

What the children have learned

The children have learned to use planning to guide their writing. They have seen how the teacher writes a report and the way she refers to her own plan, modelling for them how they should use their plans when they write. They have a real purpose for writing and they are writing from experience gained on the walk around the town.

Chapter 5

Sustaining interest in Year 3

In this chapter we cover: writing openings to stories; focusing on language to create effects; a non-chronological report; observational poetry.

In Year 3, children are revisiting many of the texts and developing further those skills learned at Key Stage 1. They are both consolidating and pushing forward as writers and a range of interesting opportunities can engage them and support their learning.

Using language to create effects with Year 3

Seeking out a stimulating purpose for writing

The teachers want the children to write openings for stories that will be used in a library display. They will read their story openings on to a tape, using sound effects if they so wish. A book of the openings will be made afterwards that will be attractively illustrated and kept together with the tape in a strong plastic wallet. It will then be placed in the school library, available for children to take home or listen to at the library listening post.

Plotting the path through the planning

The teachers have chosen two **key** objectives for this unit of work:

> Y3T3TL11: to write openings to stories or chapters linked to or arising from reading; to focus on language to create effects, e.g. building tension, suspense, creating moods, setting scenes.
> Y3T3TL2: to refer to significant aspects of the text, e.g. opening, build-up, atmosphere; and to know that language is used to create these, e.g. the use of adjectives for description.

It is the stickability of skills that the teachers really want to address, so they have selected one or two aspects of the objective to focus on that the children can catch and keep.

They have considered what the children already know about language effects in openings and what they will be learning next year. They decide to explore in depth how authors build up atmosphere in openings using just one or two of the senses; they decide on sound and sight.

The writing objective is explicitly linked to the reading objective. They want to show the children how an author sets a scene and creates an atmosphere – e.g. the techniques she uses, which words in which order and why – and then to show the children how to apply those same techniques and make those same writerly decisions in their own writing. The challenge is teaching something so well that it sticks and can be built on and expanded later on.

Talking through what it is you want to teach

The teachers' job is to work out just how the author does use language to create atmosphere in the settings and to translate these techniques into meaningful chunks that seven- and eight-year-olds can transfer independently into the context of their own stories. Four extracts from the book *The Sea Piper* by Helen Cresswell will be used to show the children models of language they can imitate and learn from. This book has been the class story.

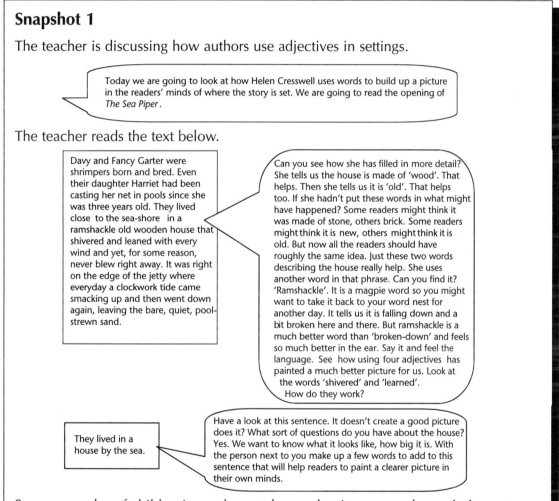

Snapshot 1

The teacher is discussing how authors use adjectives in settings.

> Today we are going to look at how Helen Cresswell uses words to build up a picture in the readers' minds of where the story is set. We are going to read the opening of *The Sea Piper*.

The teacher reads the text below.

Davy and Fancy Garter were shrimpers born and bred. Even their daughter Harriet had been casting her net in pools since she was three years old. They lived close to the sea-shore in a ramshackle old wooden house that shivered and leaned with every wind and yet, for some reason, never blew right away. It was right on the edge of the jetty where everyday a clockwork tide came smacking up and then went down again, leaving the bare, quiet, pool-strewn sand.

> Can you see how she has filled in more detail? She tells us the house is made of 'wood'. That helps. Then she tells us it is 'old'. That helps too. If she hadn't put these words in what might have happened? Some readers might think it was made of stone, others brick. Some readers might think it is new, others might think it is old. But now all the readers should have roughly the same idea. Just these two words describing the house really help. She uses another word in that phrase. Can you find it? 'Ramshackle'. It is a magpie word so you might want to take it back to your word nest for another day. It tells us it is falling down and a bit broken here and there. But ramshackle is a much better word than 'broken-down' and feels so much better in the ear. Say it and feel the language. See how using four adjectives has painted a much better picture for us. Look at the words 'shivered' and 'learned'. How do they work?

They lived in a house by the sea.

> Have a look at this sentence. It doesn't create a good picture does it? What sort of questions do you have about the house? Yes. We want to know what it looks like, how big it is. With the person next to you make up a few words to add to this sentence that will help readers to paint a clearer picture in their own minds.

Some examples of children's words are taken and written up underneath the sentence and discussed, e.g. spooky, shaking, old.

The teacher now writes on the board a series of sentences, e.g. 'She sat by the tree'. She asks the children in pairs to copy them on their whiteboards and to add adjectives to make a stronger image for the reader. She then writes up children's alternatives under each sentence and discusses the strengths.

The teacher reminds them that using effective verbs and adjectives in their settings would be a useful skill, and she will be looking out for them in their own stories when she reads their stories.

Snapshot 2

In another lesson the teacher wants to show how authors use verbs in settings to describe sounds and create a sense of atmosphere. The teacher plays some sounds from a tape she has prepared (e.g. bell, drum, cutlery falling, something that creaks) and asks the children to discuss how each sound makes them feel and what it reminds them of.

She tells the children that Helen Cresswell uses sound throughout the book to create atmosphere. She tells the children that they are going to investigate how she does it so they can use descriptions of sounds in their own writing to create atmosphere.

They read together the extract below.

The day started like any other. Fancy got up first, as she always did, slamming the shutters back more to make sure everybody else woke up than for any other reason, for it was five o'clock and black as pitch outside.

Harriet, lying in her narrow trundle bed, could hear her grumbling and waited for the moment when the door would open and the golden shaft of lamplight would fall across the wall.

One by one she heard the familiar morning noises , the rattle of the latch, the working of the old iron pump, the clatter of pots and pans. Then, in the intervals of silence, she heard the rain, pattering steadily on the roof and against the walls and windows of her tiny room.

When a writer tells us the sounds, she can really make the story come alive for us in our head. It can make us feel like we are really there.

What sounds can you see Helen Cresswell has written in this description?

Write two on your whiteboard with your partner.

What sounds does Harriet hear inside the house?

(The teacher discusses rattle, clatter and slamming.)

What sounds does Harriet hear outside the house?

(The teacher discusses silence, pattering steadily.)

These sounds give us clues about the atmosphere of the house. They make us feel a certain way. How do they make you feel? Tell your partner.

They take the reader into the scene. We can imagine hearing those sounds around us. Using sounds in our own settings and openings can really help our writing.

The teacher then says she will demonstrate how she can use this same technique in her writing. She writes the following sentences on the board and then revises them, as below.

- Some birds were in the trees overhead.
- The leaves rustled under his feet.
- Just then a car went by.

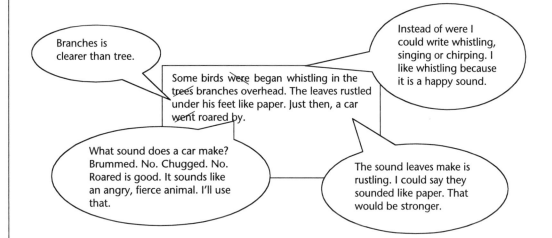

The teacher writes on the board a familiar place, e.g. the swimming pool or the playground, and the children work in pairs to write sentences describing the sounds the reader might hear. They read them out to each other on the mat and discuss how they made each other feel. One or two are written up on the board and the children discuss them in the plenary.

The teacher reminds them that the use of well chosen words to describe sounds the reader might hear is a useful skill, and she will be looking out for it in their own stories when she reads them.

Snapshot 3

The teacher further develops the children's understanding of how to use sounds to create a sense of atmosphere.

She tells them they are going to look at some more sounds today, and the class is going to start a 'Magpie word nest chart' of useful sound words. The children can add to this poster chart throughout the week. It will hang at eye level next to the whiteboard where everyone can see it.

> Do you remember the section from the book when the family return to the empty village. Today we are going to investigate how Helen Cresswell uses sounds to make the reader feel a sense of loneliness. I want this half of the class to search the first paragraph for sounds and how they make us feel and the other half to do the same with the other paragraph.

She gives them some time to search the text and discuss it. She listens to contributions from the children.

Screaming gulls is the noise of an animal. We could use barking.

She uses silence. It feels hollow

This makes it sound like singing. It is like the boats are making music. It makes me feel loneliness

Only when they drove into the shuttered village, when the wheels stopped rolling and the silence crept up on them again, did their spirits sink. To be sure, the tide flapped idly under the jetty and the gulls wheeled and screamed under the low cliffs just as they always had, but the people were missing, and they had left a silence that all the sea noises in the world could not hide.

They sat there blankly.

'We shall get used to it,' said Fancy in the end. 'It's not as if anyone likes a lot of noise.'

They fetched the cow out of the wagon, and she slid unsteadily over the cobbles. She mooed and roused a storm of indignant echoes that scattered the gulls perched on the nearby roofs. While Davy led her up to the green Fancy and Harriet saw to the hens, and it was dark before the wagon was unloaded and everything stowed and ship-shape. That night the Garters were too tired to notice that the stars were the only lights out over the bay, or to miss the soft knocking chorus of fifty boats against the sea wall.

Silence itself tells us there was no noise. Saying it creeps makes it feel like an animal. Jumped at us wouldn't sound right.

The cows mooing and the echoes makes the town seem very empty. You only hear echoes in empty places.

The teacher reminds them that she will be expecting them to use well chosen words to describe sounds in their own openings to stories.

Snapshot 4

To reinforce the lessons, the children are set homework. They are to go 'fishing for sounds' with a pen and paper. They are to go to a place and listen. Then they are to write down the sounds they hear. They are given suggestions such as the park, the local shop, the loft, the garden, the street, one of the rooms in their house. A carer is to go with them if they leave their house.

They return to school with the homework and in pairs or small groups share their 'sound catch'. Then they are to try to craft their sounds into a sentence or two.

Showing how to do it

The teacher wants to bring together all the teaching points that have been made and show how to use sound, weather, light and temperature to create a setting.

Snapshot 5

The children sit on the mat and the teacher produces a book with illustrations of a setting from *First Snow* by Kim Lewis.

The children look carefully at an illustration and have two minutes to brainstorm and list on their whiteboards as many words as they can think of to describe it. The words are gathered on a shared writing board.

> Now you have helped me to gather some ideas I am going to use them to show you how to write an atmospheric setting. Watch out for the way I use words to describe what the reader can see and hear. You need to watch for five minutes now and at the end tell me what you think works and what doesn't and where you would put a golden line under the best description. I especially want to use Helen Cresswell's idea of getting the sounds right for the reader.

The teacher begins to write in front of the children, giving a running commentary on what she is thinking as she is writing.

Sarah and her mother looked up at the sky and saw the clouds turning grey. They were low in the sky.

> Lets read that back. Hm! Sky and sky doesn't sound right. I'll keep one and write 'Sarah and her mother looked up and saw the clouds turning grey. They were low in the sky.'
>
> I'll read that back *(she reads it aloud)*. It could run together smoothly if I join the sentences like this *(she reads out as she writes)*.

Sarah and her mother looked up and saw the grey clouds hanging low in the sky. It was so cold her face was stinging and there were tears in her eyes.

> I could describe the clouds. Sarah and her mother looked up and saw grey clouds *hanging* low in the sky.
>
> (She reads it back.) Sounds good. That word 'hanging' really helps. I am going to write next about how cold it was. Something about the cold made her face sting.

Sarah and her mother looked up and saw grey clouds hanging low in the sky.

It was so cold her face was stinging and there were tears in her eyes.

As the snow began to fall the crows squawked and squealed.

Their black shapes fluttered – no – flapped across the grey sky.

> *(She reads back all of it.)* That sounds really good. Now what does she hear? I am going to borrow Helen Cresswell's idea of the noise of the seagulls but I am going to make it my own. I have had it in my 'magpie nest' all week and now I am going to take it out and use it. I think I'll say 'as the snow began to fall the crows squawked and squealed'.
>
> *(She writes as she speaks.)*
>
> As the snow began to fall the crows squawked and squealed. Their black shapes fluttered – no – flapped across the grey sky.
>
> Now let's read it back and see if we want to make changes

She reads it back and comments that it seems to work. She asks the children if they think this would create an atmosphere in the reader's mind and takes feedback asking them to say why they want to change something and how it will make it better for the reader.

She tells them she thinks it does work because it tells the reader what Sarah sees, what she feels and what she hears.

Drafting and crafting

Children are shown pictures from good quality picture books which would stimulate their writing, e.g. *Way Home* by Libby Hawthorn, *Beware Beware* by Susan Hill, *The Man Who Wanted to Live for Ever* by Selina Hastings. They must apply the techniques of choosing precise adjectives and effective verbs to create an atmosphere. They are required to write sentences describing things they see, and things they hear.

The children write in silence and then share what they have written with a response partner, referring to the golden rules of settings the teacher has displayed on the wall. The teacher expects the children to constantly loop back and re-read their own work to check for meaning and coherence.

What the children have learned

The children have used their senses and drawn on their own experiences to write a setting. They have looked closely at the work of professional authors and applied some of the ideas to their own writing. They have seen how their teacher, the expert writer, composes a setting, drafts, crafts and refines, and they have heard the conversation that goes on in the writer's head because the teacher has given a running commentary as she wrote in front of them.

Non-chronological report writing with Year 3

Snapshot 6

Year 3 teachers are having a planning session in preparation for next term's work – the autumn term. Their focus is to look at ways of improving links between the National Literacy Strategy framework and geography. The senior management team has been conducting a review of cross-curricular links. The 'carry-over' between geography and the National Literacy Strategy framework is not yet established in the school and year group leaders have been asked to do this as one of the priorities in next year's school development plan.

They have at hand the medium-term plans for geography and literacy for that term. The geography focus is 'improving the environment'. The National Literacy Strategy focus for non-fiction is in two parts: (a) information books on topics of interest; (b) non-chronological reports. There are obviously possibilities for linkage across the subject areas.

Their resources list for geography shows a wide range of resources on aspects of the environment, including a collection of books, posters, photographs, CD-ROMs and video material, including local materials. Several 'big books' are also held in stock.

Seeking out a stimulating purpose for writing

The teachers decided that a purposeful outcome of part of the geography work would be a report on classroom and playground litter and rubbish. A governor had already suggested that pupils should be involved in coming up with an improvement plan. A report would be the starting point for such a plan. They all wanted pupils to be engaged in a writing task which had a real purpose and an audience who would read, respond and, more importantly, act upon the report to secure improvement for their school.

A title was decided upon: **Litter in Brandon School – a cause for concern?**

The data and information gathered as part of the investigative approach in geography would be used as the content for the report to the governor. The structure of an information report would be taught in the literacy hour as part of the sequence for teaching writing outlined by the National Literacy Strategy. The teachers decided to invite the governor to talk to the children about the report and discuss the next steps towards an improvement plan.

Plotting the path through the planning

The teachers discuss how the work in geography can feed into the literacy hour, and vice versa. They plan when to introduce the non-fiction unit, and decide on which 'big book', other extracts and CD-ROM material to use, based on their experience of using them during the previous autumn term.

> Y3T1TL19: to locate information using contents, index, headings, subheadings, page numbers, bibliographies.
>
> Y3T1TL23: to write simple non-chronological reports from known information, e.g. from own experience or from texts read using notes made to organise and present ideas. Write for a known audience, e.g other pupils in class, teacher, parent.
>
> Y3T1SL9: to notice and investigate a range of other devices for presenting texts, e.g. captions and headings, inset text.
>
> KS2ENG1 (speaking and listening): 1, 2 and 3.
>
> KS2 GEO: geographical enquiry and skills a, b, c, d, e.

Talking through what it is you want to teach

At the beginning of this non-fiction unit the teacher writes up and explains what the objectives are – what she wants pupils to learn about these chronological reports so that they can write one themselves. Teachers know what they have to build on because pupils will already have written a number of non-fiction text types at Key Stage 1: lists, captions, letters, recounts, instructions, simple non-chronological reports and explanations. They also know that in Year 3 term 1 they will revisit the non-chronological report in more detail.

Teachers display examples of non-chronological reports on world and local environments directly linked to the focus in geography. As each text is displayed and discussed during the shared reading sessions, pupils are asked what the underlying purpose of the text is. The teacher then makes explicit the grammatical features of this text type. (This is directly linked to the sentence level objectives from the NLS Framework at Year 3 Term 1: 9, *to notice and investigate a range of other devices for presenting texts, e.g. captions and headings, inset text.*)

Snapshot 7

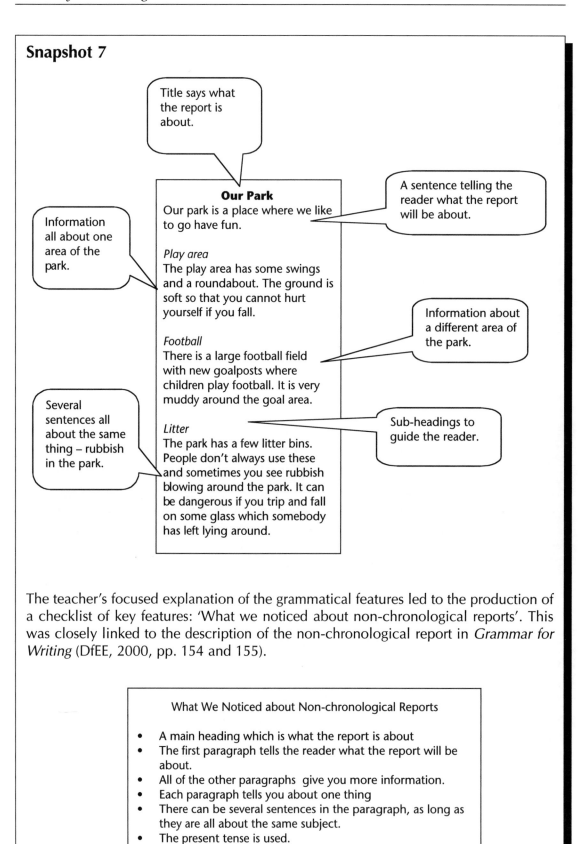

The teacher's focused explanation of the grammatical features led to the production of a checklist of key features: 'What we noticed about non-chronological reports'. This was closely linked to the description of the non-chronological report in *Grammar for Writing* (DfEE, 2000, pp. 154 and 155).

> What We Noticed about Non-chronological Reports
>
> - A main heading which is what the report is about
> - The first paragraph tells the reader what the report will be about.
> - All of the other paragraphs give you more information.
> - Each paragraph tells you about one thing
> - There can be several sentences in the paragraph, as long as they are all about the same subject.
> - The present tense is used.
> - Each sentence may contain more than one fact.

Snapshot 8 A report for the governors

By following the medium-term planning for geography, pupils have gathered together information on the amount of litter in the classroom and in the school grounds. Pupils have:

- weighed and sorted classroom rubbish, keeping a cumulative graph alongside an interactive display;
- sorted the rubbish into different types;
- collected litter in different parts of the school ground;
- produced a colour coded map of the school grounds to show where rubbish was distributed;
- observed the use of litter bins in different locations in the school grounds.

Pupils bring data, charts and notes to the literacy hour and the teacher demonstrates how to start off a report incorporating some of these facts.

The teacher wants them to write a report which includes three paragraphs: classroom litter, playground litter and use of bins.

The teacher again demonstrates part of the text, then asks the pupils to complete it. Her demonstration text has been enlarged and is on the classroom's 'working wall' section.

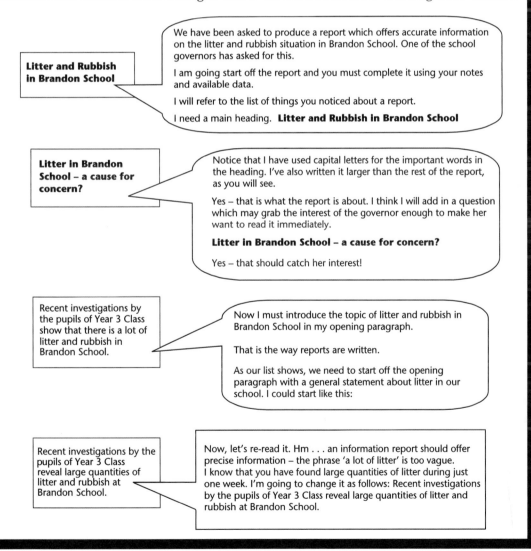

Litter and Rubbish in Brandon School

We have been asked to produce a report which offers accurate information on the litter and rubbish situation in Brandon School. One of the school governors has asked for this.

I am going start off the report and you must complete it using your notes and available data.

I will refer to the list of things you noticed about a report.

I need a main heading. **Litter and Rubbish in Brandon School**

Litter in Brandon School – a cause for concern?

Notice that I have used capital letters for the important words in the heading. I've also written it larger than the rest of the report, as you will see.

Yes – that is what the report is about. I think I will add in a question which may grab the interest of the governor enough to make her want to read it immediately.

Litter in Brandon School – a cause for concern?

Yes – that should catch her interest!

Recent investigations by the pupils of Year 3 Class show that there is a lot of litter and rubbish in Brandon School.

Now I must introduce the topic of litter and rubbish in Brandon School in my opening paragraph.

That is the way reports are written.

As our list shows, we need to start off the opening paragraph with a general statement about litter in our school. I could start like this:

Recent investigations by the pupils of Year 3 Class reveal large quantities of litter and rubbish at Brandon School.

Now, let's re-read it. Hm . . . an information report should offer precise information – the phrase 'a lot of litter' is too vague. I know that you have found large quantities of litter during just one week. I'm going to change it as follows: Recent investigations by the pupils of Year 3 Class reveal large quantities of litter and rubbish at Brandon School.

Now the teacher involves the pupils by asking for suggestions as to what each paragraph could be about.

The rubbish in the classroom bins is usually made up of : waste paper, felt tipped pens which have run out of ink and pencil shavings.

This report now needs to be more specific – which types of litter and rubbish? Let's start inside the classroom.

I would like the group who have been collecting the classroom rubbish to tell me what the next paragraph will be about. It needs to give the governor more information about what kinds of classroom rubbish have been found.

Now , how would you like to start this off – remember it must be in the present tense. Thank you – that is very clear. I know that you have a graph which could be added to your report to offer further evidence of this. You will need to write a caption for the graph which explains what it shows.

Now in pairs, use your information to write further paragraphs about what your investigations showed about rubbish and litter in our school. Refer to our 'What we noticed about non-chronological reports' poster.

The teacher then works alongside one of the less experienced groups in a guided writing session.

Drafting and crafting: responding to writing

Pupils continue with these reports as part of literacy and geography lessons. Samples of work are marked by the teacher based on the criteria of this particular text type. This is annotated to show how near the pupil is to achieving the required features as listed in 'What we noticed about non-chronological reports'.

What the children have learned

The children have seen how to construct and organise a non-chronological report. They are motivated because they know their work will be read and it has a real purpose. They have taken part in an investigation and applied the knowledge gained from it to their own writing. They have seen how their teacher writes a report and how she reads back and makes changes with the audience's needs in mind.

Poems based on observation with Year 3

Seeking out a stimulating purpose for writing

The teacher tells the class that the poem they are going to write in pairs will be presented at the monthly parents' afternoon. Their poems will be supported by observational drawings based on photographs, and material on water gathered from a CD-ROM, e.g. waterfalls, rivers, rain, storm and snow. There are links to the medium-term plan for art.

Plotting the path through the planning

The teacher focuses on the following objectives for this work:

> **Reading comprehension**
> Y3T1TL 6: to discuss choice of words and phrases that describe and create impact, e.g. powerful and expressive verbs.
>
> **Sentence level work**
> Y3T1SL 2: to take account of grammar and punctuation when reading aloud.
> Y3T1SL 3: the function of verbs.
> Y3T1SL 5: to use the term 'verb' appropriately.
>
> **Writing composition**
> Y3T1TL 13: to collect suitable words and phrases in order to write poems.

These objectives were the focus for what followed.

Talking through what you want to teach

> **Snapshot 9**
>
> We join the literacy hour just after the teacher has put up the poem 'Leaf'. The class listen intently as the teacher reads the poem twice, the second time with their eyes closed to focus on the movement verbs.
>
> **Leaf**
>
> Leaf spin
> Leaf curl
> Leaf dance
> Leaf whirl
> Leaf flutter
> Leaf furl
> Leaf tumble
> Leaf in hurly-burly
> Crumble
> Yellow-brown
> And down
> And down.
>
> John Kitching

She reads it to the class and asks questions which steer them towards the text level objectives, which are about:

- the choice and impact of particular words – in this case the choice of verbs;
- the effect of the layout (the downward journey of the leaf);
- the repetition of the last two lines which gives the effect of the leaf floating down;
- the lack of punctuation;
- the rhyming pattern.

The teacher describes these verbs as 'power packs' – words which give energy and movement to this poem. As the children note the verbs she adds them to a display entitled 'Words which "pack power" – power pack words'. She asks them to explain the difference in the movement of the leaf matched to each verb. They do this in a variety of ways, guided by the teacher, e.g. picturing the movement by comparing it to other things, such as a spinning top, sycamore 'helicopters' spinning down, water spinning down a plughole in a bath. They also use their hands to 'draw' the movement in the air.

Showing how to do it

Snapshot 10

The teacher then says that she is going to show them how to plan a poem similar to this one. Her title is 'Cat'.

She brainstorms a lists of words which describe how a cat moves, introducing the activity:

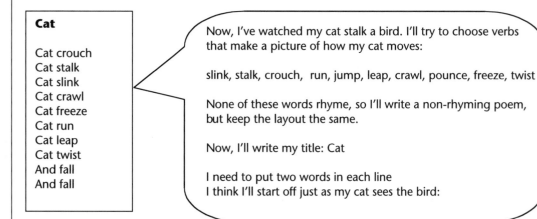

Cat

Cat crouch
Cat stalk
Cat slink
Cat crawl
Cat freeze
Cat run
Cat leap
Cat twist
And fall
And fall

Now, I've watched my cat stalk a bird. I'll try to choose verbs that make a picture of how my cat moves:

slink, stalk, crouch, run, jump, leap, crawl, pounce, freeze, twist

None of these words rhyme, so I'll write a non-rhyming poem, but keep the layout the same.

Now, I'll write my title: Cat

I need to put two words in each line
I think I'll start off just as my cat sees the bird:

Drafting and crafting

The next day pupils in pairs brainstorm a list of words which describe movement words for a waterfall, and then organise their text using 'Cat' as a model. If they wish, they can consult a thesaurus to help them with a wider range of words. They then move on to draft the poems on whiteboards first of all. After some time spent re-reading, deleting and substituting words in their poems, they come up with a finished poem.

Sharing their ideas on the whiteboards

The teacher regularly stops the class to share ideas. Several whiteboards with children's poetry on them are stacked against the big board for other children to view and comment upon. Others are displayed on a shelf until the next literacy hour, so that children can see the importance of this messy but most important aspect of writing 'in process'.

The teacher also copies a few of these to go on display, on the class literacy 'working wall'. This again affords status to the drafting and crafting aspect of writing. These are word processed over the course of the next two weeks, possibly outside the literacy hour, in the ICT suite.

Art lessons are used for observational drawings of waterfalls based on photographs of video footage or CD-ROMs to accompany more poems.

This time, the children are encouraged to choose their own forms but use 'power-packed' verbs wherever appropriate, wherever they work.

What the children have learned

The children have enjoyed playing with language. They have learned to select the best words to achieve the effect they want and they have thought about the power of a well chosen verb.

Children also need plenty of experience of creating their own forms in original poems. Work like that described above needs to be part of a broader, mixed diet of poetry writing. It supports and provides the foundation for exploratory and creative writing.

Chapter 6

Writing with confidence in Year 4

In this chapter we cover: writing character sketches and explanations.

Year 4 pupils need to develop their story writing skills by looking in detail at how different elements of story writing can be refined. In this chapter we focus on the way writing in the literacy hour can link to other subject areas in a mutually supportive way.

Writing character sketches with Year 4

Seeking out a stimulating purpose

At the heart of all good writing is having something you want to write about. The children in this classroom are being helped to get 'inside' the characters they are going to write about. By pretending to be the characters and having to describe themselves and listen to other children's descriptions they stand a better chance of building a picture in their own minds that they can write about. It is also fun and involves use of speaking and listening skills. The sort of preparation described below, where there is both drama and teacher modelling, gives the children a stimulus to write and shows them how. The collaborative nature of the work means that the children are supported and can learn about writing from each other: trying things out, being reassured their ideas work and borrowing ideas from each other to extend their own skills. The children will write letters with a character sketch in them and these will be made into a simple book and display board for the library – they will be read by other children in the school.

Plotting the path through planning

The teachers enjoyed some success last year teaching characterisation. They decide that role-play will provide a rich source of material for children to draw from. It is also an excellent opportunity for further developing their speaking and listening skills. The teachers spend part of one staff meeting analysing children's stories and setting writing targets. They find that their children describe the 'outside' of characters (what they look like, what they wear) but rarely describe personality and feelings. Adjectives were used reasonably well but descriptions of the way they move or say things are hardly ever made. They also want to get the children to think about using what the character says. It is very ambitious and they draw up a list of what they can expect from each group of children.

The cluster of objectives chosen are:

Y4T1TL2: to identify the main characteristics of the key characters, drawing on the text to justify views, and using information to predict actions.

Y4T1TL11: to write character sketches, focusing on small details to evoke sympathy or dislike.

Y4T1SL4: to identify adverbs and understand their functions in sentences through

- identifying common adverbs with the *ly* suffix and discussing their impact on the meaning of sentences;
- noticing where they occur in sentences and how they are used to qualify the meaning of verbs;
- collecting and classifying examples of adverbs, e.g. for speed, *swiftly, rapidly, sluggishly, brilliantly, dimly;*
- investigating the effects of substituting adverbs in clauses or sentences, e.g. *they left the house —ly;*
- using adverbs with greater discrimination in own writing.

Y4T1SL1: to reread own writing to check for grammatical sense (coherence) and accuracy (agreement); to identify errors and to suggest alternative constructions.

EN1KS2 4c: to use dramatic techniques to explore characters and issues (for example, hot-seating, flashback).

Snapshot 1 Investigating character sketches

There is the noise of discussion. It is the beginning of the literacy hour and children are working in their groups, each reading a different character description from well known books.

Once they have read the extract, they have to work out what the author has done to make the character description work. They have a question card to guide them:

1 Read the extract at least once
2 What do you know about the character?
3 Do you think it is a good character description?
4 What are the words or phrases which give you clues to the character's feelings and attitudes?
5 Are there any special details that help you paint a picture in your own mind?

The children return to the mat for the shared session. Each group makes lists on their mini-whiteboards and then shares their selected words and phrases with the rest of the class. The teacher has an OHT of each extract so all the children can see and begins to draw out the key features of a good character description, writing them up on a piece of sugar paper. (This has great potential for interactive whiteboards.)

Showing them how to read a text with a 'writer's eye' and a 'reader's ear'

In the following English lesson, the teacher uses an extract from a children's book to draw out in discussion some key features of an effective character description. As the shared reading unfolds, the teacher keeps reminding the children that these are techniques they can use in their own writing. She makes sure that they appreciate the underlying purpose of well crafted character sketches: giving the reader a view of someone, more than merely a word picture of how they look.

> **What she says shows us the type of character she is inside. She could say 'Get out of my way, idiot.'**
>
> **She is gentle and polite.**

> **She describes what she looks like: her height, hair, skin and noticeable features.**

> **She is hurt and embarrassed by her ears. She doesn't want to fight. Probably been teased before.**

> **She is proud and can control her feelings. Her actions show us what she is like. The author lets us work it out ourselves.**

She was the very first person I met on my very first day at Dale Road Secondary School. We bumped into each other at the door of the hall where we'd been sent to wait for our class teachers.

'Oh, sorry,' she said.

'Me too,' I said.

She was much taller than me, and quite thin. She had a bush of brown frizzy hair and pale brown skin which was dotted all over with freckles. But what you noticed straight away was her ears. They were large, and stuck out away from her head. Like bats' ears.

'My name's Lucy,' I said.

'I'm Rafaella,' she said.

I don't know what got into me. Perhaps it was the nervousness of starting a new school. Perhaps it was the way she looked down at me, a little aloof, as if I was an interesting insect miles below her.

"I can't call you *that*,' I said, bursting into loud laughter. 'I'm going to call you Earwig. Eerie-Eerie-Earwig.'

She flushed up to the roots of her hair and turned away. I could tell that tears had sprouted behind her eyelids, but she wasn't going to let me see them.

Secret Friends by Elizabeth Laird

Together they agree on a set of golden rules for writing character sketches that they must apply in their own writing when they write stories.

Golden Rules for Character Sketches

- How they look (expression).
- What they wear (e.g. hair, shoes, jewellery).
- How they move (relaxed/hurried...).
- What they do (how they respond to events).
- What they say.
- How they say it (tone, speed).

Snapshot 2 Approaching shared writing as authors

A video extract of the White Witch from the BBC video of *The Lion, the Witch and the Wardrobe* is freeze-framed on the television. There is no soundtrack. The class have been asked to write in pairs on their show-me whiteboards a description of the White Witch from this frozen moment – what she looks like and what she is wearing. This is time bonded to five minutes. When the time is up, they read their descriptions to another pair and make comments. Some of these are shared with the whole class.

The teacher going into role as the 'White Witch'

The teacher then reminds the children that a good character description will show what the character is like inside, as well as describing what she looks like. The teacher then declares that she is now going to take on the role of the White Witch and the children ask her questions about her meeting with the boy.

Some questions have been planted, including:

- What were you like when you were a child?
- What makes you happy?
- How do you feel about children?
- What makes you sad?

The teacher steps out of role and writes a letter in front of the children. The children are asked to imagine that the witch has found an injured princess. Now that the children have met the White Witch themselves, in the roleplay, they are in a position to write with vigour and authenticity and are more engaged.

Before writing the teacher makes a brief plan on the board of what will happen.

Plan

1   I am injured.
2   The White Witch approaches.
3   She lifts me on her sleigh.
4   She takes me to her castle.

The children are given the first lines of the letter:

Dear Mother,
I was in the Wild Wood yesterday when the strangest thing happened to me.
I stumbled on a fallen log and injured my leg . . .

Showing how to do it

I want a sentence to develop the scene and tell the reader where I am and what has happened. Let me rehearse the sentence. I knew my ankle was badly hurt and I would freeze to death in the wood if someone did not come to help me. It was then I saw her... No, It was then she appeared.

> I knew my ankle was badly hurt and I would freeze to death in the wood if someone did not come to help me. It was then she appeared.

(Reads it back.)

Now to describe the way she looks. And what she is wearing. (*Looks at the golden rules.*) I am going to borrow some of your ideas from earlier. 'I noticed how tall she

> I was struck by how tall she was and then I noticed first her skin. It was as white as ivory.

was first and then her skin. It was as white as ivory.' I like that. I am going to write I was struck by instead of I noticed because it gives more sense of power.

(She writes on board.)

I like the use of the simile. It is like the one Roald Dahl used for the Bloodbottler when we read *The BFG*.

Who can suggest some more detail to help the reader paint their own picture?

(Takes suggestions and says why she thinks the ideas she chooses will work.)

Let's read it back. *(Reads it back.)* Sounds good.

If we look at our golden rules it would be good if we could say how she moved.

She walked over to me. I think it needs an adverb. Look at the list on the wall. I think boldly might work. *(Writes sentence on board.)*

Now we want to see if we can show her character by what she says and how she says it. *(She points to the golden rules.)*

Let's put '"Help me," I said.' Now what would the Witch say? Write it down on your show-me boards and write how she says it too.

(The teacher discusses suggestions and chooses a sentence.)

I like yours, Catherine and Briony. '"You foolish girl!" she said icily. "I will help you but you will have to do something for me."'

Let's read it back and see if it paints a good picture in the reader's mind.

> She had small, cold , blue eyes and long black hair. Around her shoulders, she wore a silver fur coat and on her head a white crown that looked like icicles pointing upwards.

> She walked boldly over to me

> I knew my ankle was badly hurt and I would freeze to death in the wood if someone did not come to help me. It was then she appeared I noticed how tall she was first and then her skin. It was as white as ivory She had small, cold , blue eyes and long black hair. Around her shoulders, she wore a silver fur coat and on her head a white crown that looked like icicles pointing upwards. She walked boldly over to me.
>
> 'Help me,' I said.
>
> 'You foolish girl!' she said icily. 'I will help you but you will have to do something for me.'

Snapshot 3 Hot-seating for something to say

The teacher recaps what they have learned about writing a character portrait so far.

The children are put into groups of four. Each one is hot-seated by the other members of the group using a guidance card. The roles they take on may include dragon, wizard or knight.

Any question can be asked but the five questions on the guidance card must also be asked. They are given a few minutes to prepare. Each child is hot-seated for three minutes.

Example guidance card

You are a dragon

You meet an injured child in the woods or on the road.

Questions you will be asked:

What do you look like?
What makes you happy?
How do you feel about children?
What makes you sad?
What will you do with the child? Why?

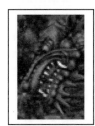

The children are then asked to write a letter as if they are the injured child. They must describe the character who finds them and what happens. Figure 6.1 shows an example.

They review each other's work, look for the features of a character sketch in the golden rules list and discuss how well it has been done.

> Dear Mother,
> I was in the wild wood yesterday when the strangest thing happened to me. I stumbled and hurt my knee on a sharp rock. I waited until dark for help, finally an old wizard approached through the dark shadowed trees. He was wearing a thick brown cloak and dragged a stubborn donkey behind him. He looked at me with his kindly old eyes, his face was winkled and grey and seemed to glow. From his chin fell a long white beard and his lips were a pale pink colour. He said, "do not be afraid, child, I shall help." He gently lifted me onto his donkey and I fell asleep. When I awoke the next morning I was in a small and cosy hut the wizard

Figure 6.1

Figure 6.1 shows one writer's lively first draft of a character sketch. He describes the old wizard's clothes and uses the adjective 'wrinkled' to give texture to his face, going on to say that it 'seemed to glow', emphasising the wizard's kindness. He has revealed the character through what the wizard says: 'do not be afraid child'. Reading back was useful to this apprentice writer because he added a simile, to make his lips 'like roses', and the adverb 'gently' to convey the way the wizard lifted the injured boy on to his already 'loaded' donkey.

What the children have learned

The children see the teacher composing in front of them and how she refers closely to the golden rules which are the markers for success. They see how she is drawing from the things they learned in shared reading from professional authors. They hear the teacher rehearsing the sentence and reading back frequently to check for cohesion. They hear and see how she changes writing, making additions, deletions and substitutions. Importantly, they hear how she is considering the needs of the audience and is always aware of the purpose of the text. The teacher models and scribes and involves the children throughout.

Writing explanations and taking notes with Year 4

Seeking out a stimulating purpose

The teachers want to make a close link between the non-fiction genre of writing they are teaching in English and their science topic: 'Keeping warm', based on QCA science unit 4c. They identify a mutually supporting link between the experiments on conductors and insulators they will be covering in science and explanation writing in English. The children will be presented with a challenge related to the real lives of elderly people – how to keep warm in winter. A leaflet is to be written on keeping warm. The work they do in science will provide the material for their writing in English.

The teacher has already approached the local organiser of Help the Aged and will arrange an opportunity for the children to talk about and present their finished leaflet to her when she visits the school.

Plotting the path through planning

The children have already been taught how to locate information, take notes and use them.

> Y4T2TL18: to mark extracts by annotating and by selecting key headings, words or sentences, or, alternatively, noting these.
> Y4T2TL21: to make short notes, e.g. by abbreviating ideas, selecting key words, listing or in diagrammatic form.
> T4T2TL25: to write explanations of a process, using conventions identified through reading.

Snapshot 4

On the Monday of the week of the English unit on writing explanations, the children do a science experiment on conduction. A piece of frozen butter is stuck to the handles of a wooden and a metal spoon. The bowls of the spoons are then put in a beaker of warm water. The children observe what happens. After the experiment the teacher takes the children to the hall to explain why the butter on the metal handle melted first.

The teacher explains how heat is passed through the materials in different ways because of the different arrangement of the molecules. Children pretend to be the molecules of the different spoon handles. The free moving metal spoon molecules stand up in an untidy line and pass a red rubber ball, representing heat, along the 'human spoon' with their hands. The more rigid wooden spoon molecules make a line of triangles – three children joined by holding three wooden rulers – and must pass the red rubber ball without using their hands. The mime demonstrates how the metal molecules carry heat away more quickly, causing the butter on the metal spoon to melt. The children now have some knowledge to draw on when they write. They produce a diagrammatic version of the two sets of molecules 'in action'.

Talking through what you want to teach

Snapshot 5

It is Tuesday's shared reading in the literacy hour and the children are investigating how an explanation text is constructed.

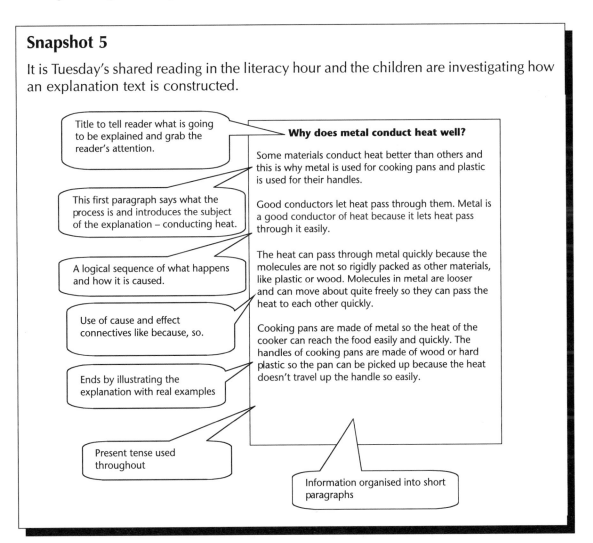

Title to tell reader what is going to be explained and grab the reader's attention.

This first paragraph says what the process is and introduces the subject of the explanation – conducting heat.

A logical sequence of what happens and how it is caused.

Use of cause and effect connectives like because, so.

Ends by illustrating the explanation with real examples

Present tense used throughout

Information organised into short paragraphs

Why does metal conduct heat well?

Some materials conduct heat better than others and this is why metal is used for cooking pans and plastic is used for their handles.

Good conductors let heat pass through them. Metal is a good conductor of heat because it lets heat pass through it easily.

The heat can pass through metal quickly because the molecules are not so rigidly packed as other materials, like plastic or wood. Molecules in metal are looser and can move about quite freely so they can pass the heat to each other quickly.

Cooking pans are made of metal so the heat of the cooker can reach the food easily and quickly. The handles of cooking pans are made of wood or hard plastic so the pan can be picked up because the heat doesn't travel up the handle so easily.

A set of golden rules for writing explanations is written up and made into a poster for the children to refer to when they come to write and revise their own explanations.

> **Golden Rules of Explanation Writing**
>
> - Title tells the reader what is going to be explained.
> - First paragraph introduces the reader to what is going to be explained.
> - There is a logical sequence to what happens.
> - Uses connectives like so, because, since.
> - Uses the present tense.
> - Organised into paragraphs.

Showing how to do it

In the next literacy hour **and** science lesson the children are reminded how to take notes. According to their ability, they are given texts to read on insulation (e.g. from the DIY shop, the health centre and science scheme books), which tell the children about how to use layers of clothing to keep warm, how a vacuum flask works, how to keep food warm or cold, how birds and other animals keep warm, how to keep a house warm and why certain materials act as insulators.

Equipped with this background reading and the practical experience of the science experiments, they are ready to write their own explanation using the conventions which govern the genre.

Showing how to write

Snapshot 6

The children are presented with the challenge – they must produce a leaflet explaining to elderly people in their community how to keep warm in winter. They bring their notes from the science lesson where they have explored simple materials which are good insulators.

We need to think of a title for the leaflet that tells the reader what is going to be explained. Can you write a title down on your whiteboards?

You have one minute.

(The children write in pairs and the teacher constructs a title from their suggestions.)

I think this works because it clearly tells the reader what is going to be explained.

I need a first paragraph that introduces the explanation for the reader and grabs their attention. This winter there are several things – what about easy things – you can do to keep yourself warm.

> **Keeping Warm**

> **Keeping Warm**
> This winter there are several easy things you can do to keep yourself warm.

Look at your notes and decide on one really useful thing our audience, elderly people – can do. *(The teacher takes suggestions from the children.)* I think I will choose to write my next paragraph about keeping their bodies warm. So the whole paragraph is going to be about that.

If you wear several layers of clothes then you will feel warmer. This works because I am using the connectives 'if' and 'then' together which is useful in explanations.

> If you wear several layers of clothes then you will feel warmer.

Now I want to explain why. Can anybody Tell me why? Think back to your Science experiments and look at your notes. *(Teacher listens to children's contributions.)* I am going to write 'This is because' – that because conjunction is very useful in explanations – 'layers of clothing trap air. Layers of air keep you warm because air is a good insulator and heat does not go through it quickly.'

> This is because layers of clothing trap air. Layers of air keep you warm because air is a good insulator and heat does not go through it quickly.

Let's read it back. I think travel is a better verb than go so I will change it. I also think we should put 'between them' after 'This is because layers of clothing trap air'.

> This is because layers of clothing trap air between them. Layers of air keep you warm because air is a good insulator and heat does not g̶o̶ travel through it quickly.

Can you write the next sentence about why they should wear woollen clothes and slippers. Work with your partner on whiteboards. Use your notes and rehearse the sentences before you write.

The children show the teacher the sentences they have composed and some are read out to another pair. They are discussed by the teacher and some ideas are used which comply with the teaching points about explanations the teacher is trying to make.

Drafting and crafting

The children go off and work on their own. They draft out their explanations. Staged deadlines are set to motivate children and give a sense of achievement. At intervals they share their work with other children and evaluate it against the 'golden rules', making appropriate suggestions and improvements. The teacher works with a guided writing group. The writing is completed in science time.

What they have learned

The children have written from a strong foundation. They know about insulation from their science investigations and they have first-hand experience to draw from. They have something to say in their writing. They have seen the conventions of explanation writing and they have clear success criteria to guide their attempts. The teacher has shown them the process of writing, demonstrating how to gather ideas, rehearse, read back and improve sentences as they are written. They have seen her struggle with the composition of sentences, discuss why she has made changes and consider the needs of the audience. They have revisited note taking and reinforced that skill. They are supported in this writing. Drama, well managed talk and discussing their work before it is completed have all helped them.

Y4T2 Explanation Genre	Whole-class word and sentence level	Whole-class text level	Guided reading/writing	Independent work	Plenary	Links to science
Monday	Word level work investigating what happens to words ending in 'f' when suffixes are added		Guided reading with one group analysing an explanation text	Group activities investigating suffixes	Children report back what they have learned about suffixes	Conduction experiment, mime and diagrams
Tuesday	Shared reading of explanation text about conductors to identify key features of explanation genre		Guided reading with one group analysing an explanation text	Group activities investigating suffixes	Guided reading group report back what they have learned about explanation genre	Insulation experiments
Wednesday	Word level work investigating what happens to words ending in 'f' when suffixes are added	Remind children how to take notes and demonstrate	Guided reading with one group taking notes from texts about how to insulate houses	Notetaking from texts about how to insulate houses	Children report back what they have learned about insulating houses	Notes taken about insulation from selected texts
Thursday	Demonstration writing of explanation genre How elderly people can keep themselves warm during winter		Guided writing with one group reinforcing structural features of explanation and planning explanation	In pairs, draft some ideas for an explanation of how to keep warm	Children share ideas about the content, order and language features they are going to use for their explanation	Time to continue with explanation writing and how to construct a supporting diagram for the explanation
Friday	Whole-class revision of selected children's explanation writing on overhead projector. Features of explanation genre reinforced		Guided writing with one group refining what has been written so far and developing quality of sentences	Working individually, write explanation of how to keep warm. Revise writing with a partner. Additional time will be needed to complete the leaflet.	Children reflect on what they have learned about explanations, any difficulties and successes they had and when they might use it in the future	

Y4T2TL18: to mark extracts by annotating and by selecting key headings words or sentences, or, alternatively, noting these.
Y4T2TL21 to make short notes, e.g. by abbreviating ideas, selecting key words, listing or in diagrammatic form.
T4T2TL25 to write explanations of a process, using conventions identified through reading.
T4T2WL5 to investigate what happens to words ending in 'f' when suffixes are added.

Chapter 7

Lifting off in writing in Year 5

In this chapter we cover: play writing and diary writing.

Children are bringing together a range of writing skills and are beginning to deploy them successfully in a variety of creative contexts. Cross-curricular links offer the content to support and stimulate their interest.

A Year 5 blitz diary: writing a diary with a cross-curricular link

Seeking out a stimulating purpose

The children have been asked to write some diaries to accompany a display in the community centre.

The theme of the display is 'Our community during the Second World War'. They will be writing as if they are children in the war. The finished work will be collected by a community leader – there is a deadline for this work. The teachers have prepared a unit of work that does at least three things for the children:

- stimulates them;
- shows them how to use particular writing conventions of a diary;
- links neatly to the work in history.

The use of drama in the unit is of key importance.

Plotting the path through planning

To prepare them for the diary writing, the children will learn in history lessons about the bombing of Britain during the Second World War. They will refer to the QCA primary scheme of work: History Unit 9. What was it like for children in the Second World War. This would provide them with the background for the drama experience. The teachers considered various ways to make the history lessons about the blitz come to life. Ideas included:

- inviting an elderly resident of the community who remembers the blitz to talk to the children;
- visiting an Anderson shelter that a neighbour has preserved in the back garden;
- using suitable video footage from programmes like 1940s House or World at War;
- photographs;
- a debate about the reasons for and against bombing of civilians;

- making posters about what to do in the event of an air-raid which would link to the National Literacy Strategy objective for writing instructional texts;
- the teacher in role instructing them what they must do in the event of an air raid.

The objectives they would bundle together were:

Y5T1TL24: Write recounts based on subject, topic or personal experiences for (a) close friend and (b) an unknown reader, e.g. an account of a field trip, a match, a historical event.

Y5T1TL21: Identify the features of recounted texts such as sports reports, diaries, police reports, including
- introduction to orientate reader;
- chronological sequence;
- supporting illustrations;
- degree of formality adopted;
- use of connectives, e.g. first.

KS2EN1 4a: to create, adapt and sustain different roles, individually and in groups.

KS2EN1 b: to use dramatic techniques to explore characters and issues.

KS2HIS 11b: Britain since 1930.

The children had visited diary writing at least once before in Year 4 but the teachers decided they would first need to revisit these skills and understandings, and 'ratchet up' the quality of writing, setting high expectations.

Talking through what you want to teach

Snapshot 1 Grabbing their interest

The teacher tells the children the objectives for the unit of work and for the day which have been written on the wall. She has brought in some diaries that she has collected, and shows them to the children. They discuss who owns a diary. Many children have been given children's personal organisers and mention them, volunteering what they do with them. The teacher puts children into six small groups and gives each group one of three extracts from diaries: *The Diary of Anne Frank* (first four paragraphs of the entry for Saturday 20 June 1942), *The Story of Tracey Beaker* by Jacqueline Wilson and *The Diary of Adrian Mole Aged 13¾* by Sue Townsend. The groups are set questions. What is the diary extract about? Who has written it? Why has it been written? How is it different from other types of writing? After discussing in their group, they make two large groups, each with a person from Anne Frank, Tracey Beaker and Adrian Mole in them, and they exchange what they have found out after reading each extract to the others in their group.

The groups are brought together and their ideas collected by the teacher. Some key factors about reports are caught on a 'Golden rules of diary writing' poster.

Golden Rules of Diary Writing

- Usually about things that have happened in the past – recently.
- Often tells the story of an episode in the writer's life.
- Written as if talking to someone.

- Written in the first person – uses I and we, my, me.
- Intimate – talks about feelings.
- Uses connectives of time.
- Has an introduction to direct the reader.

Snapshot 2 Analysing a diary recount text

The teacher displays an OHT of an extract from *Blitz: The Diary of Edie Benson, London 1940–41*, by Vince Cross. This is discussed and annotated to see if it has the features of a diary.

Introduction to signpost the reader

She talks about her feelings, like talking to a friend

She tells an episode in her life

Uses descriptive and figurative language

She has a conversation with the diary – as if the diary is a living friend – Sorts out her thoughts

Uses slang and idioms – not fully formal

Reveals she is a willing, mature character who gets on with things even if she doesn't like it.

Sunday, 8th September

I'm trying to write this in the Anderson. There isn't much light and I'm all scrunched up in a corner so who knows whether I'll be able to make sense of it later on. It's half past six in the evening, but we've been here an hour or so already.

I feel small and scared and dog-tired. None of us got much sleep last night. In fact, I think yesterday was the worst day of my life . . .

Later in the evening, when Mum had gone off on duty, we could hear the drone of planes overhead more or less all the time. It's horrible. You feel the butterflies building up in your stomach till it almost becomes painful. I could see Shirl's fingers. The nails were bitten back hard, and her two hands were gripped together, the fingers sliding backwards and forwards over each other. It was about three o' clock when a stick of three bombs dropped closer than we'd ever heard before. They came through the air with a sound like the tearing of a curtain, and the explosions shook the ground. Chamberlain was beside himself with fear, past barking now, just trembling uncontrollably and whining pitifully . . .

Thursday, 12th September

It's the same every night now. Bombs and more bombs, and they're getting closer. A house got hit in Sandringham Road last night. That's one over from Summerfield. Sometimes I feel frightened and sometimes it makes me angry. The Germans don't seem to care who they might kill. What's going through the minds of the pilots when they drop their bombs? Haven't they got wives and families? So how can they try to kill other people's children?

I mean, I understand why they might want to bomb a factory that's making guns. I can even understand why they might try to hit a power station. But what difference does it make to the war if they kill Mum, or Tom? Or Me? . . .

Life's gone a bit funny. The best time to sleep is in the early morning, and because Mum and Dad both have to be out quite often at night, they try to catch a bit of kip during the daytime. So I seem to end up doing even more dishes and tidying up than normal. *And* most of the shopping too! Even Tom lends a hand from time to time. Mum says it's our bit towards the war effort, and put that way we can't grumble, can we?

Children need many opportunities to see how a writer composes and refines a passage of writing. It is not obvious to them and it takes some time for us as teachers to bring to the surface and explain clearly what exactly it is that we do in our heads as we compose. It all seems to happen so quickly and naturally. But we need to slow the process and break it down so that the children can see and hear what is going on.

Snapshot 3 Showing them how to write

The children are shown an edited video of the Blitz from *The World at War* by the BBC. The teacher models her diary entry on the board for the children.

I want now to tell this episode of my life so I will use the past tense. It's a recount really. I want to gather my ideas first. I was on my way home from choir practice when the siren went but the bombs were falling before I could get home and I saw the explosions and heard the noises. This gives me a little plan which I can build on.

*(She rehearses the first sentence aloud and writes it, reminding the children that it is important to consider the audience's need to know **where** and **when** the event happened. The teacher then reads it back and suggests it would strengthen the diary if some reported speech of what the priest said were added. She asks for ideas of what the priest might have said and then shows how she makes it into reported speech and weaves it into the diary recount.)*

Let's read it back. *(She makes some changes.)* That sounds great. You see, like a potter I've shaved off some bits and pushed some new bits in.

What else might we use? Let's look at our golden rules poster. Let's put in a sentence about how she is feeling. *(She rehearses the next sentences and writes.)*

Now let's read it back and check it says just what we want it to say. *(She now invites children to contribute the next sentence on whiteboards.)*

> It was about 8 o'clock last night and I was on my way home from the choir practice. Father O'Reilly told Billy Yates off for making rude noises. *Father O'Reilly said Billy enjoyed playing the fool too much and he would be talking to his mother about it at mass the next day.*
>
> I was laughing about it to myself when the sirens started. That wiped the smile off my face.
>
> Almost straight away I heard the dull thuds of the exploding bombs not far away.

> I felt sorry for the people over in Westville where the bombs were exploding. What if there were children there walking home from church right now – just like me?

Snapshot 4 Something really rich to write about

The children have been told that they will be taking part in a drama this week and that there will be an air raid while they are at school so they will need to carry their gas masks around with them. They all have shoeboxes covered in brown paper with string attached to represent gas masks. The teacher and the assistants have dressed up in 1940s clothes to add to the atmosphere. The children have each been issued with a folded A4 'diary' dated 1940 for them to record their feelings and make any notes during the drama.

They are just about to begin lessons when a loud recording of an air raid siren is played. A teaching assistant dressed as an air raid warden bursts in to hurry them outside, where they are led across the playground, the sound of the siren playing on a portable cassette recorder accompanying the crocodile of children.

They reach a room that has been specially prepared for the morning (e.g. the staff room, the art room, the library). The windows have been blacked out. The children sit on the floor and the teacher calls out the register. One child is missing. The air raid warden rushes out to find the child who has been asked to wait with the secretary. She returns with the child and the teacher demands to know where she has been. She says she was left in the toilet. The siren ends and there is a few seconds of silence. Then the assistant plays the sound of explosions.

When the explosions end, the teacher in role gives a 1940s' style lesson in the air raid shelter. The assistant brings round some orange juice and a biscuit. The teacher continues for a while until the all clear is sounded.

Throughout the drama children have been given slots of time to record any thoughts or feelings so that they can draw off them during the writing of their diary later that day, after the teacher has modelled the beginning of her own diary entry. Throughout their writing time, children are encouraged to read back, check against the golden rules and read each other's work. The teacher works with two specific groups to help them as they write in a guided writing context. The drafts are then written neatly on lightly browned paper to represent their diaries, recounting the day they had an air raid at school.

Spotlight on planning

The teacher identified the English learning objectives and adhered closely to them throughout the sequence of focused lessons. The conventional internal structure of the literacy hour won't work on the day of the drama, so some alterations were made and the history time was 'blended in' with the literacy. The teachers made some intelligent modifications to the literacy hour, but the key teaching strategies and focus on objectives has been retained.

What the children have learned

One of the reasons many children find writing difficult is because the moment of writing involves the bringing together of several skills at once, and they rarely get it right first time. The teacher has demonstrated how she prepares her writing first, then writes, and then goes back to check for things to add, delete, substitute or move. The children were shown how to go back and change their writing, and they knew what they were looking for because they had a set of 'golden rules' to guide them. There is an emphasis on reading back their own work as they write to check for meaning and coherence rather than waiting until the end.

Writing plays with Year 5

Seeking out a stimulating purpose

The teachers know that the children have a rich seam of **prior knowledge** to tap into when they teach the children to write playscripts. Children have been inventing plots, dialogue and action for dramas with their friends ever since they learned to talk. With their plastic action figures and dolls they have been directing their own thrillers, soap operas and action movies on their living room floors.

Knowing that they are going to write a **play** with a historical background should motivate them in their research and note-taking in history lessons. When the children are told that they will be performing themselves and watching classmates act out their plays they are excited and motivated. Their writing will have a purpose because their work will be published in the form of a performance and perhaps an audio tape to go in the library, accompanied by a class book of the scripts.

Plotting the path through planning

The teachers have objectives from the National Literacy Framework to teach and they want to link them to another area of the curriculum to provide a context and background information for the playwriting.

> Y5T1TL19: to annotate a section of playscript as a preparation for performance, taking into account pace movement, gesture and delivery of lines, and the needs of the audience.
> Y5T1TL5: to understand dramatic conventions, including the conventions of scripting, e.g. stage directions, asides; how character can be communicated in words and gestures; how tension can be built up through pace, silences and delivery.
> Y5T1TL18: to write own playscript, applying conventions learned from reading, including production notes.
> KS2EN1 (speaking and listening) 4a: to create, adapt and sustain different roles, individually and in groups.
> KS2HISTORY10 (Britain in Tudor times) 5c: communicate their knowledge of history in a variety of ways.

Teachers decide on learning objectives and exactly what skills and techniques they want the children to have learned about scriptwriting and the process of writing.

The children will have to write a play that:

- takes place in a Tudor school;
- or happens at the time of a plague;
- or involves crime and justice.

Talking through what you want to teach

The teacher creates the space for them to discuss and share what they already know about playscripts, aware that a few children are supplying most of the information and mentally recording those who are saying little. Lots of important points come up during the discussion and are caught on the whiteboard by the teaching assistant. An extract from a play is read together during shared reading and the purpose and presentation of stage directions are discussed.

Snapshot 5

The children are given an enlarged photocopied extract from a published play script for children, e.g. scene 11 from *Charlie and the Chocolate Factory*, adapted by Richard George. They note down on their small whiteboards the key features of play scripts and rejoin the teacher, who scribes the following set of golden rules.

Golden Rules for Writing Playscripts

- Have two or three characters.
- New speaker on a new line.
- Character's name on left followed by colon.
- Stage directions in italics and brackets.
- Use stage directions to show *how something is said*.
- Use stage directions to tell you *where acting is happening*.
- Use stage directions to tell you *how someone is moving*.

These are written up as a poster and pinned to the wall. They have been generated through an investigation, and will serve as a reminder for the children while they are writing and form success criteria to guide their drafting of each other's work.

Showing how to do it

Snapshot 6

During a history lesson the children watched a video about Henry VIII closing the monasteries. Notes were made and they will draw on this information as they are composing a play script with stage directions. At the beginning of the lesson, the teacher writes: *Today we are going to learn how to compose a script and practise using stage directions.*

The teacher recaps the golden rules of writing scripts and refers to the poster of 'Golden rules' on the wall next to the board. The beginning of the scene is already prepared on the board. The teacher discusses it, before developing the scene in shared writing.

This tells actors where scene takes place and gives directions for lighting. It tells the actors where they should be positioned. Can you imagine it?

This tells actors how they should say the line

This tells the actors what they should do as they say the line.

The monastery is dark and a candle flickers on the table. MONK and ABBOT are sitting on chairs round the table.
Monk: *(Hushed voice)* We must leave before they come and take us away, Abbot.
Abbot: I will not leave this monastery. It is my home.
Monk: *(Leaning across table)* But they have burned down other monasteries and terrible things have happened to the monks. Henry hates us and will show us no mercy.
Abbot: *(Rising from seat, furiously)* I am not scared of him! If we leave then who will look after the poor, where will the sick go.

Now let's think how we can move the scene on. Discuss with the person next to you what we might write next. Write it on your whiteboards and show me. *(Teacher reads boards.)* I like Amy's and Dan's idea. The stage direction moves the story on and it tells the actors clearly what to do and gives instructions for a noise. That's something we can add to our golden rules *(Writes on poster 'Use stage directions to tell when to use sound effects'.)* Tom and Gemma's words are menacing.

I am going to write the next line. Let me gather my ideas. . . . I think the Monk is younger and scared. I think the Abbot is scared too but doesn't show it and comforts the Monk. I'll have the Monk saying: 'What are we going to do? They might kill us' and the Abbot would comfort him. I'll rehearse the sentence before I write. 'Hush my son' . . . no . . . just 'Hush. Be brave. They cannot hurt us.' I will put a stage direction to show how it is said: gently.

There is a sharp knock. MONK and (ABBOT freeze and look at each other) SOLDIER: (from offstage) Open up by order of the King. You are under arrest.

MONK: What are we going to do? They might kill us?

ABBOT: *(gently)* Hush. Be brave. They cannot hurt us. They wouldn't dare.

Let's read it back and see if it works well and see if we have followed all the golden rules. *(Reads back and refers to the poster.)* I think I'll add 'They wouldn't dare.' It tells the audience why the Abbot is calm. It makes the audience question if the soldiers would dare. Good. Now you write the next three lines with your partner on your whiteboards.

Drafting and crafting

During history lessons the children work in pairs to research and write a leaflet about crime and punishment, health and medicine, or education in Tudor times. They use this information to make up a short play scene. One literacy hour is spent in the hall, where the children can discuss and experiment with acting out their scene, and make some notes. During a later literacy lesson they write their scene on their own. When they read each other's work they use small cards to guide their discussion, like those below.

I have	
Used stage directions to say where the action is happening	
Written who is speaking on the left hand side	
Put a colon after speaker's name	
Put a new speaker on a new line	
Written how the person is speaking or how they are moving in brackets	
Used (pause) to heighten tension	
Used stage directions to show how something is said	
Used stage directions to show how someone moves	

> Read your script to another group and ask them these questions:
>
> - **Do you know where the scene takes place?**
> - **What works well (characters, lines, directions...) ?**
> - **What other information would you need to act the scene out?**
> - **Have you ideas for words to add or change?**

Another way of teaching children to write playscripts is to provide them with a story that they can convert to a playscript. This provides more support and allows them to focus on techniques of scriptwriting. Figure 7.1 is an example of a story, related to the Tudor history topic, and a child's script using the skills learned in the unit.

The extract in Figure 7.1 is from a nine-year-old's first draft of a playscript. It can be seen that she has understood many of the golden rules of writing scripts and has used them effectively. She shows awareness of the reader's needs throughout. A list of characters is given at the top of her work. She begins the script by giving the readers stage directions telling them how the characters should enter, and sets the scene. She uses the characters' names on the left, followed by a colon. In places she has composed and written a line and then read back and decided to add in more information to enrich the script. For example, in line 5 she added 'But *(pause)*' for dramatic effect as Thomas begins to realise something is wrong with his father.

Characters:
Thomas
Mother
Emily
Landlord

(Thomas enters a dusty house mumbling to himself and sees Mother crying)

Thomas: Mother. What's wrong?
Mother: *(sobbing)* I have some terrible news.
Thomas: What? Has something bad happened?
Mother: Yes. I am afraid so. Your father has died of the plague *(crying even more)*
Thomas: But *(pause)*... where is he? *(starting to cry)*
Mother: The men have already taken him away and buried him. Don't tell Emily. Just wait a bit.
(Emily enters)
(Emily whistling to herself, then suddenly sees Mother kneeling on the rug and Thomas with her)
Emily: What's happened? Where's Father?
Mother: He's gone. He's died. He's caught the plague.
Emily: What...!!
(Landlord enters)
Landlord: I heard the news about your husband.
Mother: Yes. It's terrible *(starts crying. Thomas puts his arm around his mother)*
Thomas: What are you doing here?
Landlord: You have to leave your house.
Mother, Emily, Thomas: *(shout)* What?

Figure 7.1

What the children have learned

The children have learned to use some of the content from their history lessons in a play. They have learned how important it is to use the correct conventions and layout of play scripts. They have thought carefully about the needs of their audience and they have drafted in the light of responses from readers of their work. This approach is mutually beneficial for history and literacy, each giving the other a fuller life.

Chapter 8

Broadening horizons in Year 6

In this chapter we cover: the use of metaphor and simile and developing the conventions of newspaper reports.

By Year 6 the children are becoming increasingly independent. However, they still need a lot of focused support and stimulating contexts in which to thrive.

Metaphor writing in Year 5/6

Seeking out a stimulating purpose

The pupils have been allocated a central area of the library in which to mount their own display of work. This term the focus is on poetry and they are going to write two-line metaphor poems which they will stick on the front of differently sized boxes. Inside each box is the object the poem describes. Other children will be invited to read the poem and 'open the box'.

Plotting a path through planning

The teacher wants the children to be stretched by extending their understanding and use of similes and metaphors so that they understand the subtle differences between them

> Y5T1TL17: to write metaphors from original ideas or similes.
> Y5T2TL10: to understand the differences between literal and figurative language.
> Y6T1TL10: to write own poems experimenting with personification.
> Y6T2TL3: to recognize multiple layers of meaning, e.g. through figurative language.

Talking through what it is you want to teach

Snapshot 1 Introducing metaphors: metaphors that sell cars!

The pupils have been asked to bring in a collection of glossy pictures of new cars. The children in small groups share these, reading the text to go with the pictures and generally giving their preferences for the car they are most impressed with.

The teacher has asked them to jot down on Post-it notes what they like best about the cars – colour, design, speed and so on. Five minutes later, group representatives collect them and stick them on the class whiteboard.

Explaining to the class the purpose of this activity

The teacher explains that he is going to create powerful pictures or images which are often used in advertising to sell products. He is going to do this by writing a simile, then changing it into a metaphor. The NLS definition of a metaphor is written on the whiteboard.

> **Simile:** where the writer creates an image in the readers' minds by comparing a subject to something else.
>
> **Metaphor:** where the writer writes about something as if it were really something else.

The teacher selects a Post-it which describes the colour of the car as gold.

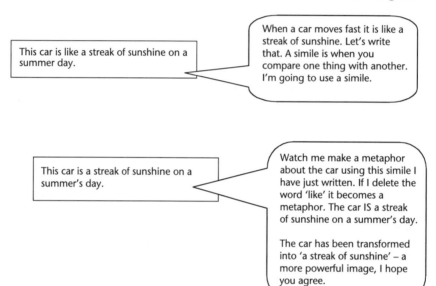

This car is like a streak of sunshine on a summer day.

When a car moves fast it is like a streak of sunshine. Let's write that. A simile is when you compare one thing with another. I'm going to use a simile.

This car is a streak of sunshine on a summer's day.

Watch me make a metaphor about the car using this simile I have just written. If I delete the word 'like' it becomes a metaphor. The car IS a streak of sunshine on a summer's day.

The car has been transformed into 'a streak of sunshine' – a more powerful image, I hope you agree.

The teacher takes another Post-it note which mentions speed and writes a second simile.

This car is like a flash of lightning on a dark summer's evening

The teacher then asks the children to transform the simile into a metaphor, which they can do very easily.

This car is a flash of lightning on a dark summer's evening.

The children are told that some car manufacturers even give their cars animal names, so the whole car is a metaphor. A Ford Mustang is named after a wild horse. Then there are the names of big cats used by car manufacturers: panther, cougar and jaguar. Then the teacher shows an advert for a Jaguar car which displays a picture of a jaguar and goes on to say:

This car has an engine which purrs along motorways and roars into action at traffic lights – which were the verbs I used which describe cats? Write down these verbs on your whiteboards.

Snapshot 2 A multisensory approach to writing metaphors

The teacher has a collection of objects in front of her and she selects one of these: a spiky coloured shell.

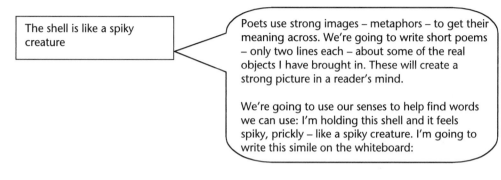

The shell is like a spiky creature

> Poets use strong images – metaphors – to get their meaning across. We're going to write short poems – only two lines each – about some of the real objects I have brought in. These will create a strong picture in a reader's mind.
>
> We're going to use our senses to help find words we can use: I'm holding this shell and it feels spiky, prickly – like a spiky creature. I'm going to write this simile on the whiteboard:

The shell is a spiky creature

> Now I am going to delete 'like' and create a metaphor:

The shell is a spiky creature from another world.

> I'm going to add these words "from another world' to make the image more interesting, because the shell did originate from another world under the sea.
>
> Now I am going to pass this shell to a few people to feel the entrance to the shell so you can give me some words which your eyes and the feel of your fingertips make you think of.

Drafting and crafting

They come up with the words shiny, smooth, glossy.

Starting with the words 'Its inside is like a . . .', she asks for contributions:

Its inside is like a shiny ice rink.

The children are asked to change this into a metaphor:

Its inside is a shiny ice rink.

The children add another image by using the words 'inviting you to slide inside'.

The completed pair of metaphors are then read:

The shell is a spiky creature from another world.
Its inside is a shiny ice-rink inviting you to slide inside.

She asks pairs of children to write pairs of similes based on what they see, feel, hear and smell about one of the objects she hands out. For example:

- a scented rose;
- a smooth pebble;
- a piece of uncut glass;
- a dried poppy head;
- a set of wind chimes;
- several differently coloured crystals.

These similes are then turned into metaphors by deleting the word 'like'. The metaphors are typed up on the computer during the week and pictures from clip-art attached. These are pasted into a simple book by the teaching assistant and displayed in the library.

Now that they have been introduced to metaphors in action, they are given a selection of poems which use metaphor and asked to identify them. They all refer to the definition of a metaphor which is written on the wall.

> Metaphor: where the writer writes about something as if it were really something else.
>
> From *Grammar for Writing* (DfEE 2000)

This time they are readers using a 'writerly eye' to scan for metaphors.

Children spot and write down a selection on their whiteboards and bring them to the next literacy hour's whole-class session to share with the teacher.

Good examples of poems to use, which can be found in a collection published by Ginn and titled *The World's Stage*, are:

- 'The highwayman', by Alfred Noyes;
- 'The beach', by W. Hart-Smith;
- 'City lights', by Margaret Greaves;
- 'Charlotte's dog', by Kit Wright;
- 'Cleaning ladies', by Kit Wright.

The metaphors the children will find offer patterns of thinking that they can use in their own writing, e.g. 'The moon was a ghostly galleon', 'The wind was a torrent of darkness'.

What the children have learned from this activity

The teacher introduces metaphor through advertising because it is a powerful and familiar image to many of the children. They will have seen advertising hoardings and noticed whole-page ads in magazines or heard car advertisements on radio and seen them on TV. What the teacher is doing is making explicit for the children the power of metaphor to create an image that helps to sell a product.

The difference between a simile and a metaphor has been made obvious by the teacher demonstrating the writing of both in front of the children. They are placed in a more powerful position as writers when they have been shown how to do it first. The multisensory activity allowed them to explore this further. Investigating metaphors in poetry made it more explicit how effective these language devices are.

They have seen and heard at first hand a teacher using her senses to help to create word pictures. The multi-sensory approach is interesting for the children. The writing demonstration and teacher talk offered the children a clear model to proceed from, which they could adhere to or manipulate as they wished. The creative urges of children were encouraged by the teacher providing a stimulus, **then** showing how to draft and craft their writing.

A journey into journalism: teaching Year 6 to use the conventions of journalism

Seeking out a stimulating purpose

The children are going to write a newspaper which will be delivered free to all classrooms and put on the school Internet site. They will learn a range of skills during this unit on journalism in order to write newspaper articles of a high standard that will be both interesting and in the interests of the readers.

Plotting a path through the planning

The Year 6 team planned this unit of work back in the summer. It was clear that objectives from the literacy framework, from speaking and listening and from other subjects could all be rolled into a coherent longer unit of work that didn't always strictly follow the regular pattern of the literacy hour. After careful consideration, it was decided that intelligent modifications to the usual structures of the literacy hour would be justified during a five- to seven-day period, as would some creative timetabling on the publication morning. This would lead to important gains made in cross-curricular links, speaking and listening, motivation and understanding of the writing process as long as key learning objectives were clearly identified, delivered and assessed.

The objectives are:

> Y6T1TL16: to use the styles and conventions of journalism to report on real or imagined events.
> Y6T1TL15: to develop a journalistic style through considering what is of public interest in events, the interest of the reader, selection and presentation of information.
> Y6T1SL5: to form complex sentences by, for example, using different connecting devices, reading back sentences for clarity of meaning and adjusting as necessary, evaluating which links work best, exploring how meaning is affected by the sequence and structure of clauses.
> KS2EN1 2c: to recall and represent important features of an argument, talk, reading, radio or television programme, film.
> KS2EN1 3: to talk effectively as members of a group, pupils should be taught to (a) make contributions relevant to the topic and take turns in discussion, (b) qualify or justify what they think after listening to others' questions or accounts, (c) deal politely with opposing points of view and enable discussion to move on.

The children have already visited newspaper report writing at least once before in Year 4. The teachers decided they would first need to revisit these skills and understandings and then 'ratchet up' the quality of writing and set high expectations.

Talking through what you want to teach

Snapshot 3 Grabbing their interest

The first lesson of the unit has barely begun. The children have been told the objectives for the unit and the teacher is now holding a pack of Pokemon trading cards in his hand, describing his son's collection. Without warning, the teaching assistant, well known to the children, her face wrapped in a football scarf and a flat cap on her head, bursts through the door, plucks the cards from the teacher's hand, and then walks out, leaving the class laughing and surprised. The teacher explains that the teaching assistant was in role!

Pairs of children then draw up a list of what they remember about how to construct a newspaper report. This provides an assessment of what they already know about newspaper report writing. The teacher uses this to begin a list of golden rules for writing newspaper reports.

Searching a shared text

When this is done, a report about a similar incident is used as shared text and the teacher begins to annotate it to highlight the key features of a newspaper report. Having just written their own version of a 'Pokemon snatch', the children approach the text as authors asking the question: 'Just how is it meant to be done, then?'

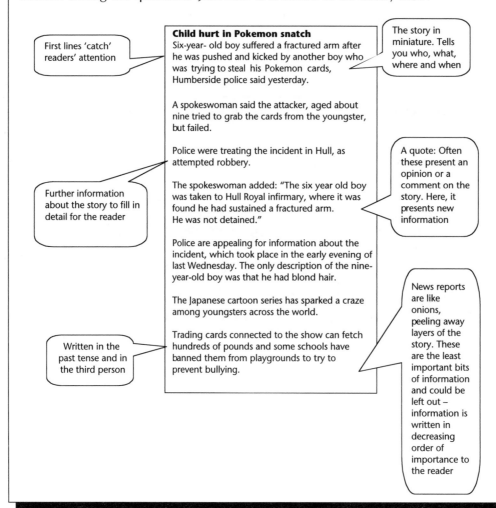

First lines 'catch' readers' attention

Child hurt in Pokemon snatch
Six-year-old boy suffered a fractured arm after he was pushed and kicked by another boy who was trying to steal his Pokemon cards, Humberside police said yesterday.

The story in miniature. Tells you who, what, where and when

A spokeswoman said the attacker, aged about nine tried to grab the cards from the youngster, but failed.

Police were treating the incident in Hull, as attempted robbery.

Further information about the story to fill in detail for the reader

The spokeswoman added: "The six year old boy was taken to Hull Royal infirmary, where it was found he had sustained a fractured arm. He was not detained."

A quote: Often these present an opinion or a comment on the story. Here, it presents new information

Police are appealing for information about the incident, which took place in the early evening of last Wednesday. The only description of the nine-year-old boy was that he had blond hair.

The Japanese cartoon series has sparked a craze among youngsters across the world.

Written in the past tense and in the third person

Trading cards connected to the show can fetch hundreds of pounds and some schools have banned them from playgrounds to try to prevent bullying.

News reports are like onions, peeling away layers of the story. These are the least important bits of information and could be left out – information is written in decreasing order of importance to the reader

The teacher then adds to their previous 'golden rules'. These will provide a compass for the children to navigate their own writing by. They will be their notes while writing and their reference during revision.

Golden Rules for Writing Newspaper Reports

- Written in past tense.
- Written in third person.
- Who, what, where, when in the first paragraph: mini-story.
- Often has a quote.
- No opinions – impartial.
- Most important things first, least important things last.

Showing how to do it

Children need to be shown how to write a newspaper report before they have a go at writing one themselves. They have been working on relative clauses in sentence-level work. The teacher now moves into a different role for the children. Instead of being the leader of an investigation into the way sentences work and the way newspaper reports work, she becomes a modeller of writing. She shows them how to weld together all the many elements that have been discussed to let the children see how an expert writer's mind works to produce a newspaper report.

Snapshot 4 Writing in front of the children

The teacher brings a shopping bag with bananas and a realistic plastic spider in it. He tells them that he is about to give them an experience which will give them ideas for their next newspaper report. He tells them that they will never believe what is in the shopping bag. He produces the bananas followed by the spider – now the children are hooked! The shock of the spider has grabbed their attention.

It is a true story that a pensioner found a tarantula in her shopping bag after a visit to the supermarket. The teacher explains that he had read a report of this in the local newspaper. He begins to write it up on large flip chart paper, and gradually involves the children, discussing and integrating their ideas into the story. He refers throughout to the 'golden rules for writing newspaper reports' they made together earlier in the week; this is the class's measure of success.

Let's put a catchy headline.

I want the first lines to grab the reader's attention and to give the story in a nutshell. The reader will want to know where it was and when. I think something like 'A pensioner was scared to death.' No, I know. 'A local pensioner got the shock of her life' and I'll say when 'yesterday'. Now let's see what that looks like. *(Writes, speaking out loud as pen moves across the page.)*

Spider Shocks Shopper

A pensioner got the shock of her life yesterday

I think that grabs the attention but I need to say why. I need to mention the spider. 'A local pensioner got the shock of her life yesterday when a tarantula crawled out of the bottom of her shopping bag' *(Writes it on board.)*

Have I answered the reader's probable questions of who, what, where and when and given the story in a nutshell? Yes.

Now, look back at the Pokemon story. The next paragraph gives same story in more detail. *(Looks at notes.)* I'll give her name, the name of the supermarket and information about how the spider got in her bag. What about 'Mrs Joan Smith saw the spider crawl out of her shopping bag across the kitchen table after her weekly trip to Supershopper's supermarket.' Sounds good. *(Writes it on the board.)*

Let's read it back. I think the reader will want to know her age so I will insert that after her name *(adds in age)*. Any other details the reader needs to know? Yes, I'll put where the supermarket is *(inserts location)*. Right, let's read it back to see if it says just what we want it to. *(Reads back whole report so far.)*

Now for the next paragraph. Let's gather ideas of what we want to put in it. With a partner decide what you think should go into it and how you would construct the sentence. *(Children talk together and offer suggestions. Teacher listens to ideas.)* You said: 'The tarantaula had been hiding in the bananas and then crawled into her shopping bag.' What about 'The tarantula had been hiding in the crate and crawled into her shopping bag when she bought a bunch of bananas,' and then add a quote.

(Teacher begins to write on board and then stops.) Hang on! I know. If I change the order of the sentence around it might sound better. What about a relative clause? *(Writes as she talks.)*

The tarantula, which had been hiding in the crate...crawled...no, jumped, we've used crawled a lot and it is good to use variety...into her shopping bag When she

---

A local pensioner got the shock of her life yesterday when a tarantula crawled out of the bottom of her shopping bag

---

Mrs Joan Smith saw the spider crawl out of her shopping bag and across the kitchen table after her weekly trip to Supershopper's supermarket

---

Mrs Joan Smith, 74, saw the spider crawl out of her shopping bag across the kitchen table after her weekly trip to Supershopper's, High Street, Winchester.

The tarantula, which had been hiding in the crate, crawled jumped into her shopping bag when she bought a bunch of bananas. Mrs Jones said: 'I was so scared I called the police. I will never eat bananas again.'

bought a bunch of bananas.' That has got an interesting relative clause. Remember, having a variety of short and long sentences makes writing interesting. I think this relative clause here works. Do you?

Now to add the quote. Mrs Jones said: 'I was so scared I called the police. I will never eat bananas again.'

Let's read it back. *(Reads back whole report adding in any punctuation and word changes.)*

Spider Shocks Shopper

A local pensioner got the shock of her life when a tarantula crawled out of the bottom of her shopping bag.

Mrs Joan Smith, 74, saw the spider crawl out of her shopping bag across the kitchen table after her weekly trip to Supershopper's, Winchester.

The tarantula, which had been hiding in the crate, jumped into her shopping bag when she bought a bunch of bananas.

Mrs Jones said: 'I was so scared I called the police. I will never eat bananas again.'

Snapshot 5 A purpose for writing

Now that the children have been shown how to write a newspaper report and have been given very clear guidelines, they need an opportunity to write themselves. To provide purpose and stimulus, the children have been told they are to pretend they are going to the local police station for the regular weekly briefing on local crime. They will see a two-minute video of a man (a friend of the teacher) talking about his car being broken into. The children are engaged.

They are given a grid with four sections to help them take notes, with the headings:

- What and when – the crime.
- Who – the victim.
- Who – the criminals.
- Where – the location.

They watch the video three times and compare their notes with those of partners to help them gather the information they need. After this, they pretend they are back in the newsroom and, in pairs, they write the first draft of their news report.

Drafting and crafting

There are many references to revision and editing of work throughout the National Literacy Strategy framework. It is important to encourage the children to ask themselves some questions about their work. These might include:

	Yes	No
Is the information in a logical order – does it hang together?		
Are there any bits of information in the wrong place?		
Are there any essential bits of information missing?		
Should any bits of information be put in a different place?		
Have I used the best sentence types to get the job done?		
Should I change some sentence types to get a better variety?		
Have I chosen the best words to get the job done?		

Pupils have to consider the purpose of the writing, what effect they want to have on the reader and just how well they have done it. This stepping outside of themselves to look, as if they had the eyes of the reader, is difficult and children need to be trained to do this.

Snapshot 6 Whole-class revision

Two children have worked together on composing a *first* draft of their newspaper report. They have written directly on to a transparency that is then shared with the class on an overhead projector. The report is well written, especially for a first attempt, but the young writers can be extended with some guidance from the teacher and their peers. With the children's agreement, the teacher discusses some changes that might enhance their newspaper report. There is constant reference to the golden rules made earlier in the week.

The boys have done well to include in a nutshell what, when and who in the first paragraph but it needs to be reorganised for more clarity.

There is some information here that is not really very important and does not add to the news story. Some words here may be considered opinion rather than fact. The children agree that the words 'special', 'precious' and 'comfy' are unnecessary and could be deleted.

The boys refer back to the golden rules of writing newspaper reports and see they have to add in a quote from the victim.

The precise time could come later (if it is needed at all) as could the detail about the suspects. The boys need to be shown that there are other ways of organising a sentence to tell where the crime happened.

Brackets would not normally be used in the first paragraph of a newspaper report.

The description of the suspects now has to incorporate the information deleted from the first paragraph.

Figure 8.1

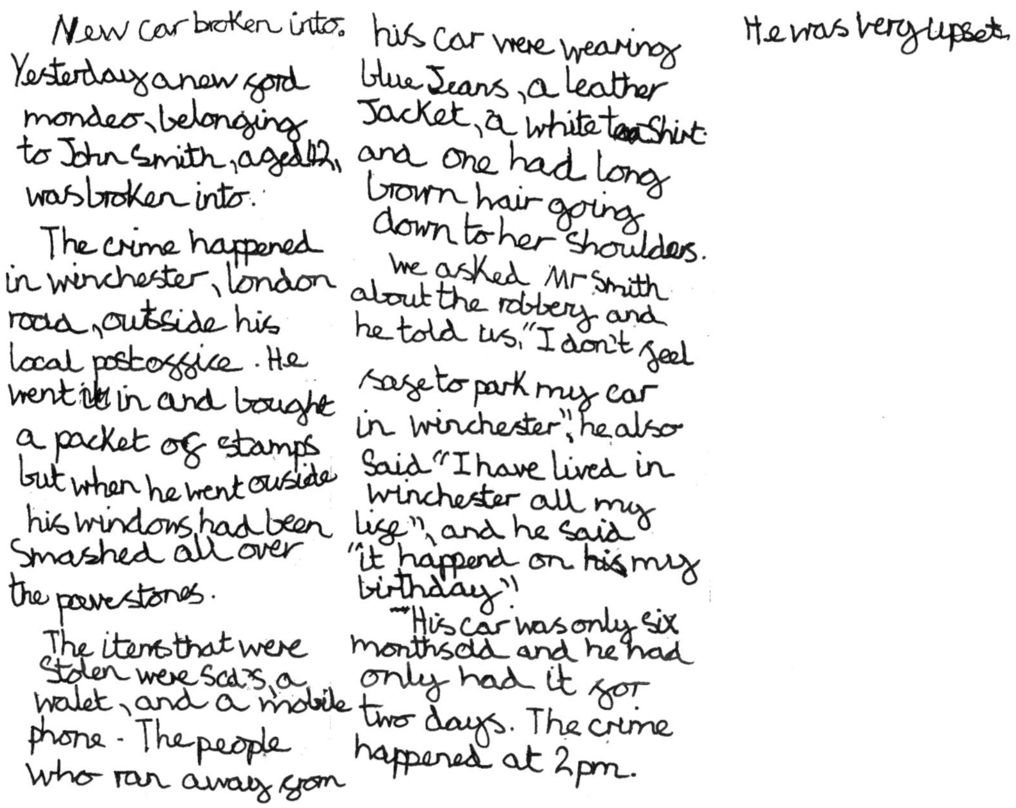

New car broken into.
Yesterday a new ford
mondeo, belonging
to John Smith, aged 42,
was broken into.

The crime happened
in winchester, london
road, outside his
local postoffice. He
went in and bought
a packet of stamps
but when he went outside
his windows had been
smashed all over
the pave stones.

The items that were
stolen were cd's, a
walet, and a mobile
phone. The people
who ran away from

his car were wearing
blue Jeans, a leather
Jacket, a white teeshirt
and one had long
brown hair going
down to her shoulders.
We asked Mr Smith
about the robbery and
he told us, "I don't feel
safe to park my car
in winchester", he also
said "I have lived in
winchester all my
life", and he said
"it happend on his my
birthday."
"His car was only six
months old and he had
only had it for
two days. The crime
happened at 2 pm.

He was very upset.

Figure 8.2

In his second draft (Figure 8.2), the writer has done well to organise the report into four clearly defined sections: the story in a nutshell; details of how the crime happened; a description of the criminals; and the victim's reaction, with some quotes. A headline has been added and some of the suggestions made to refine his first draft have been taken on board. More work needs to be done on the presentation of the quotes, and this might provide a useful teaching point in subsequent lessons or guided writing sessions. The newspaper report now has a tighter structure and the 'tune' of newspaper reports is more firmly established. There is much to praise here and some starting points for further extension.

Snapshot 7 Reporting a balanced view that is in the public's interest

The next step in the unit is to raise the issue of balance. The teachers prime two children to pretend to be the two boys involved in a fight and another child to role-play their teacher. They are given some details on a grid to refer to and then the rest of the class hot-seats them and asks them questions which they answer in role.

Billy Cruncher (child)	Mr Lens (teacher)	James Jones (child)
He's always annoying me. In class he was pinching my ruler when I needed it. And he called me a nasty word. I won't repeat it. We were playing football and then I tackled him and then he just started crying and he hit me first.	I saw Jones crying – he's only a small lad you know – and when I went over Cruncher was standing there with a bruise on his arm. Cruncher and Jones had been playing football. I know that Jones is a quiet lad and it is quite unlike him to hit anyone, especially Cruncher, who is one of the biggest lads in the school, and a well known trouble maker. Jones had a cut on his ankle. Both boys will stay in at dinner to talk it over.	I was playing football when Smith came over and kicked me in the leg. I hit him a bit hard on the arm. He had been nasty to me earlier today and wouldn't let me borrow his ruler. I told him he was nasty during lessons. That's why he hit me. He is just a big bully.

The teacher shows a prepared, very unbalanced report and the class discuss why it is not in the public's interest to use this report.

Cruncher Bashes Small Kid

A small boy was badly beaten up in the playground yesterday by a bully. The boy, who was playing football, was approached by a well known troublemaker, Billy Cruncher, and was savagely kicked in the leg. James Jones, 10, was attacked because he had been sticking up for himself earlier in the day when Cruncher, who is one of the biggest boys in the school, refused to lend James a ruler. James Jones was treated for serious injuries to his ankle. Mr Lens, who was at the scene of the fight, said, 'Cruncher is a well known troublemaker.'

The children then write with the help of the notes and the problems of balance are discussed.

Figure 8.3 shows a girl's well structured and well balanced newspaper report presenting both Billy Cruncher's and James Jones's versions of the fight in an impartial way. She tells the story in a nutshell in the first paragraph and then goes on to give details of the fight, followed by both boys' explanations. It ends with a comment from the teacher, which is the least important piece of information for the reader and can be easily edited. She has used the 'tune' of newspaper language and included a relative clause in the fourth paragraph. IT is well suited to this genre of writing. She was able to add, delete and replace words, phrases and sentences as she wrote directly on to the screen, and then emerge at the end of the lesson with a neat copy of her article.

To develop this idea of responsibility to the public, the children are given some information about a petrol tanker spilling petrol into a nearby river. They have to use a range of sources, written and prepared by the teacher (police report, eye-witness report, conservation spokesperson and petrol company spokesperson), to write a balanced report on the incident. The group uses all these reports to construct their newspaper in the ICT suite.

Yesterday, at _____ _____ Primary School, there was a fight on the playground. Billy Cruncher and James Jones were both hurt with miner injuries. Billy Cruncher, aged 10, was left with a bruise on his arm where James had hit him. James had a cut on his ankle where he had been tackled playing football. Cruncher claimed that James had taken his ruler and swore at him during lesson	time. He said it was an accident and he did not mean to trip him up. He told the press "We were playing football and then I tackled him and then he just started crying and he hit me first." James, who believed that it was not an accident, thought that Cruncher had tripped him up and did it for revenge. "He is just a big bully that's why he kicked me." James said, aged 10 as well. Mr Lens , who was at the	scene when the incident occurred , said "both boys will stay in at lunch time to discuss what has Happened."

Figure 8.3

What the children have learned

The teacher has linked the writing closely to the structure they discussed in the shared reading. He writes in front of the children and explains what is going on in his mind as he writes through a running commentary. He models making choices and shows the children the struggle that is involved in forming and choosing just the right sentence structure you need. He manages to tie in complex sentences, which they have been discussing in sentence-level work, and shows them being used for a real purpose. He is reading back and modelling the way to create cohesion, so the writing flows smoothly together. The children are involved and there is a flexible use of demonstration, scribing and supported composition to maximise the involvement of children.

The children are being shown how to revise and the golden rules guide them. They are seeing the teacher rework a piece of writing by adding, replacing and deleting. They see the teacher constantly reading back and trying to see the writing with the eye of the reader. They hear the teacher asking the questions listed above, and they hear the teacher listening to the sound of the 'flow' of the writing as he reads aloud. The children, having seen and heard the expert writer at work, can apply the same techniques to their own writing.

Involving parents at Foundation Stage and Key Stage 1

Speaking and listening, and how these help writing

Parents act as natural models for their children while they are developing as speakers and listeners. From the moment of birth parents talk to their babies as if their babies can understand them. Their offspring are learning fast – about the rhythms, patterns and nuances of the spoken word.

Through eye contact and talk, 'real' conversations and games can take place where the parent encourages her baby to respond to her in some way, from a smile, to a coo or a gurgle.

Before too long the baby is experimenting with sounds, then words; their meaning is guessed by the parent at first but over time comes closer and closer to a recognisable word – supported by the parent repeating that word over and over. These words begin to be linked together into spoken sentences.

What is key to making meaning as a speaker is also important in constructing meaning as a writer – the construction of the sentence.

No parent has lessons in this, but parents should know that making time to have fun, listen and converse with their children from the beginning is the first essential building block for the literacy that underpins and supports writing.

Reading: how this helps to prepare children for writing

Sharing books together has become normal for most parents and children, part of the bonding process as well as a powerful learning tool for future readers – the pictures and print on a page can unlock an experience which is intensely pleasurable for young children.

Books can transport them to another place, e.g. a dark and lonely wood where three young owls wait in some desperation for their mother to return (Owl Babies by Martin Waddell). Books can entertain them through the world of nursery rhymes – Jack and Jill and Three Blind Mice – scare them (on their parent's lap) as they hear the giant's roar of 'Fee, fi, fo, fum' from the fairytale Jack and the Beanstalk and inform them about their bodies as in All About Me by Debbie Mackinnon. As the child watches the parent turn the page, then turns the pages independently, then 'reads' because the words have been learned off by heart, an important message is coming over – that books are good fun, that the black marks offer a message which can be repeated over and over, every time the book is shared. This is a rock solid experience for the child becoming a reader herself and serves as a second building block for literacy.

As a listener, then a 'reader', the child is also widening her vocabulary and developing an implicit awareness of writing 'making sense' through the choice and ordering of words within the sentence, aided by the use of punctuation. The way the parent reads – pausing at full stops, raising her voice for a question, showing surprise when an exclamation mark is used – teaches children about the way punctuation works to aid meaning. Explicit teaching about the grammar of writing will come later as part of their primary experience in school, but the reading diet and continued exposure to books in a shared experience at home are of crucial importance to their development as writers in the future.

Writing: improved information about writing for parents

The normal development of their children as writers, as represented in the chart below, may not be known by parents. Lack of information about the typical development of young writers may lead to parents expecting their children to write 'correctly', i.e. to produce correct spelling, recognisable handwriting and accurate punctuation from the beginning. Children will experience mixed messages about writing if parents are ill-informed – what they are writing in school may not match what parents expect to see.

Mixed messages like these do not augur well for children's early days as experimental writers enjoying writing.

Typical development of young writers

What a child can do	What it looks like
Linear	~~~/mmm~
Separate symbols	toⅡot∂l6
Increasing repertoire	MƧChot
Initial sound match	c
Beginning and end sounds	cd
Middle sound picked up	cld
Auditory-visual extension	cald
Visual recall	called

This may be further compounded by a playgroup or nursery experience of too much copy writing. Young writers may be unwilling to 'have a go' at independent writing because it will look far inferior (they believe) to copied writing, and it may take some time to persuade the children to 'have a go' as independent writers. Writing independently in a risk-free environment with a sense of purpose and vitality is essential for all stages of writing, and in the Reception and early years classroom is vital if this third building block for literacy is to form a secure base.

Display children's attempts at writing, sometimes with it written below in 'book writing'. The 'translation' of children's emergent or experimental writing into book writing validates the writing, showing parents that children know that writing is about making messages, for someone else or themselves, and that it is okay to 'have a go', even if the writing has a long way to go before anyone can read it!

An information sheet on early writing is a useful way to show parents what young children write and the stages they may pass through. Schools can easily produce their own based on pupils' own writing. These can be displayed in a big book in the entrance of the school or as a wall display, with a smaller version as an advice leaflet to go home.

Appendix 2

Writing at the Foundation Stage: using recent QCA guidance for supporting the development of young writers

QCA has produced the useful *Curriculum Guidance for the Foundation Stage* (for children aged three to five), which takes the form of 'stepping stones' towards the early learning goals, which most children should achieve by the end of foundation stage (the end of the primary school reception year).

The approach to writing in the 'Communication, language and literacy' section (page 44) offers suggestions which match up with the 'snapshot' scenarios outlined in this book. Expectations are clearly outlined.

The 'Teaching' section (page 46) expects practitioners to 'encourage the children to read and write in a variety of play and role-play situations that match their interests and stimulate dialogue, activity and thinking. Children will learn about the different purposes of writing by seeing practitioners write for real purposes such as making lists, greetings cards, books to recall a visit or event, and labels for displays and models.'

Speaking and listening skills

The importance of speaking and listening skills and their links to thinking skills are made explicit throughout the whole document, supporting the notion that all reading and writing skills float on a sea of talk.

Writing with and for children

The following guidance on page 65 of the foundation document gives a clear guide to what practitioners should do, with clear links to the National Literacy Strategy's objectives for writing:

- Write stories, poems and non-fiction texts with children.
- When writing, talk about what you are doing and why, and talk through some of your decision-making on the way, such as what to write, choice of words and order. Continually re-read the writing to provide a good model for children when they write.

- Encourage children to use their ability to hear the sounds at various points in words in their writing.
- Encourage children to re-read their writing as they write.
- Provide materials and opportunities for children to initiate their writing in their play, as well as creating purposes for independent and group writing.

Here are some more examples drawn from across the curriculum, with the practitioner demonstrating writing in front of the children:

- **PSE.** Taking turns, ask their advice on playing a game and write up the agreed rules, which they then follow.
- **Communication, language and literacy.** Ask them what labels will be needed for the pet shop role-play area. Write them on cards in front of the children and get the children to place them as appropriate.
- **Mathematical development.** Ask for advice on how to fill a bottle with dry sand. Write this up as a set of numbered instructions and place by the sand tray or mount on a card.
- **Knowledge and understanding of the world.** When planning a visit, ask for their advice for a 'code of conduct' for use when, for example, walking through a wood (no running; no shouting; stand still and listen). Take this with you on the visit as a reminder.
- **Physical development.** Ask for advice from the children on how to hammer in a nail. Write it up as instructions.
- **Creative development.** Ask for advice on how to fix a pot to a box. Write it up as instructions.

'Less prepared' pupils

Children who are 'better prepared', i.e. have been fortunate enough to have experienced a literate and interested home environment, are likely to thrive on what has been laid out in the documentation above. However, 'less prepared' children need more than this.

Marie Clay, the founder of the Reading Recovery programme for children who have fallen behind their peers in both reading and writing skills, coined the term 'less prepared' some years ago and it neatly sums up the unfortunate position that many children may experience on entry to playgroup/nursery setting.

Whatever the setting, practitioners have to ensure that rich experiences of early literacy acquisition are planned and delivered if these pupils are to have any chance to make up for what they have missed in their home environment. This is their entitlement.

Marie Clay believes that the less prepared groups need as much challenge, more thought, more time, more attention and twice as many learning opportunities as the well prepared.

She suggests a planned programme of the following essential ingredients:

- More listening to and acting out of stories.
- Doubling up of writing explorations.
- Hearing and singing rhymes and songs more often than their fortunate classmates who have been there and done that.
- Massive opportunities to talk with a supportive, attentive, tutoring adult.

(Adapted from Clay, 1998)

Identifying the 'less prepared' group

Careful thought needs to be given to how to identify this group. The most useful tool is ongoing formative assessment conducted while children are at play on the range of activities as laid out in the foundation stage document.

As speaking and listening are so central to the development of literacy skills, this is a key indicator of future success and children must be assessed on their progress through 'fly-on the-wall' observations while at play or by setting up a small group activity where a child's number and quality of contributions can be noted. The ability to hear, say and repeat rhymes is an important factor in phonological awareness, and is part of this assessment.

Increasingly, exposure to books during this stage will offer assessment opportunities on the level of their knowledge of how print works in books, e.g. how it conveys meaning, has directionality, is ordered into separate words – and also how books are organised, e.g. front cover, pages in sequence, pictures offer clues to meaning etc. The way a child handles a book is a key indicator of future success.

Finally, practitioners should note how children respond to a writing task linked to play. Watching children writing, collecting in what they are doing, talking about their writing with them and analysing attempts at handwriting and applying any phonic knowledge they have acquired to the writing task – all offer a glimpse of a young writer at work. In the case of the 'less prepared' group, formative assessment is crucial to knowing what to do in a 'next steps' approach. The useful checklist below forms part of the Early Literacy Support material for teachers recently published by the DfES (2001b).

Checklist for early writing

- Pen to paper.
- Makes marks on paper.
- Attempts to write letter strings.
- Writes from left to right.
- Writes strings of recognisable letters.
- Writes letters which correspond to phonemes in sentence.
- Writes some known words.
- Starts to write clusters of letters.
- Leaves spaces.
- Leaves spaces between words.
- Begins to use capital letters appropriately.
- Reads the story/sentence back accurately.

Writing control

- Is right-handed/left-handed.
- Has a conventional pencil grip.
- Starts to write in the correct place.

Response to writing

- Reads back, attempting to use 1-1 (matching each spoken word by pointing the finger at the written word as it is spoken).
- When reading back writing, maintains sense and meaning.
- Adds to writing to develop, extend and clarify the meaning.

Thirty ways to improve boys' writing

Boys can achieve in writing. The challenge is to find the key that will unlock their potential. There is nothing surprising for either teachers or parents, or boys themselves, in the reports over the past few years that in British primary schools boys have been doing less well than girls in writing. In 2001, fewer than half of all boys sitting the Key Stage 2 writing SAT achieved Level 4 – the level that indicates they are prepared to cope competently with the writing demands across the Key Stage 3 curriculum.

Among the most insistent reasons that have been offered to explain boys' underachievement in writing are the six listed below.

- **Active lessons.** Learning to write can be a sedentary and passive experience. Boys respond to active lessons where they are involved in quality oral work, problem-solving and working together. Boys respond to active lessons and strong enthusiastic teaching (Can Do Better, QCA, 1998).
- **Maturity.** Boys seem to mature later and enter school outperformed by girls in reading, writing, perseverance, attention span and ability to play and communicate. Boys do not catch up later and it is a myth that maturity alone will take care of any differences in achievement between boys and girls.
- **Expectations.** There is substantial evidence from a range of research projects and reports that teachers have had lower expectations of boys. Boys are marked more severely and criticised in the classroom more than girls. Teachers criticise boys more frequently, openly and directly than they do girls. Ofsted (1993) found that boys receive more open and direct criticism for weaknesses in written work than girls.
- **Self-esteem.** For many there is a learned and compounded sense of failure and low self-esteem; boys fill up the bottom groups and special educational needs registers. Boys occupy a larger proportion of the category just above special needs. Children with low self-esteem are unlikely to succeed.
- **English is a feminised subject at school.** Most teachers of English in primary schools are female and most English subject managers are female. Boys may not find role models in school. Boys' sense of their own male identity will have an impact on their learning.
- **Role models.** Boys are more likely to see their mothers, sisters and other significant females in their household reading and writing. Mothers, rather than fathers, tend to read with children and help them with their homework. Fathers are themselves products of male role models who were more likely to play football with them than read or write.

We can begin to release boys' potential in writing by focusing on what we have control over: the classroom, the curriculum, the quality of the lesson and the strength of the teaching.

Thirty ways to raise the achievement of both boys and girls in writing

These are listed in random order and represent good classroom practice relevant for all pupils.

1   Show enthusiasm in your writing lessons.
2   Ensure writing has a purpose and audience. Boys do not always see the point of writing, so devise real purposes whenever possible, e.g. a book in the library, a letter, a display.
3   Teach them to re-read their writing as they do it. At intervals in the lesson, ask them to put their pencils down and re-read what they have just written.
4   Address spelling and handwriting. These are of high importance to children and insecurity or poor skills will hamper competence in composition.
5   Use guided writing to teach boys to write at the point of composition, directing them in structured activities, focusing on components and how language works in sentences.
6   Use shared writing flexibly. This is the main instrument to raise standards. Use demonstration, scribing and supported composition with whiteboards and discussion to help bring them on.
7   Write collaboratively. Use supported composition and elsewhere to bounce ideas off each other and work in a collaborative way with a variety of other children designated by the teacher.
8   Develop discussion around writing. Develop highly focused talk about writing. Model how to take part in this speaking and listening context . Boys perform well in well managed and structured contexts for talk. They are likely to learn from each other and clarify their own understandings and ideas about writing.
9   Value the 'action' writing they do write – but move them on. Boys often write stories that reflect the cartoons and video games they love. See the positive aspects of this but teach them how to develop more sophisticated narrative structures and description.
10   Drama is active and interesting. It can develop higher-level thinking skills and emotional responses which benefit writing
11   Persist with 'rewriting'. Boys do not like to redraft but persist with it. Remember, they don't need to rewrite everything.
12   Use the computer – both in dedicated English lessons and across the curriculum. Put it in your plans.
13   Link writing with other curriculum areas. In this way they will see the purpose and we can teach writing in other subjects, drawing off what was learned in English.
14   Use writing frames.
15   Write often. Ensure they have a lot of opportunities to practise and apply the skills they have learned. Consider their 'writing mileage' across the curriculum and check they have enough time to succeed.
16   Use formative assessment to set writing targets. Short next step targets that can be achieved in a relatively short space of time can motivate children. Share the specific target with them and perhaps write it on their 'writing target card'. Make the target accessible to them so they own it. Show them how to meet it. Praise them when they succeed.
17   Detailed planning based on assessment. You are teaching the children, not the literacy hour, so use the literacy hour to meet the identified needs of your children.
18   Share clear objectives, so that the children know what they are doing, why they are doing it and how it will help them.

19   Break longer tasks into series of smaller steps. For example, ask them to write a historical report paragraph by paragraph, stopping them as they go to discuss how well they have done.

20   Time bond tasks. Instead of saying 'Write some sentences', say 'I want you to write the next two sentences with your partner and you have four minutes to do it in.'

21   Clear outcomes. Tell children exactly what you expect in their writing, e.g. 'In your opening I expect . . .'.

22   Time out. Give children a minute to discuss with a partner your shared writing or the work of a professional author, and then ask them to tell you what they understand or what they want more clarification on.

23   Pace. Ensure there is a pace that matches the stage of the lesson. Speed up and slow down as appropriate.

24   Give explicit instructions, and check the boys understand them.

25   Decide who works with whom. Boy/girl partnerships seem to pay off.

26   Decide where they sit.

27   Expect. Hold and communicate high expectations.

28   Praise frequently, whenever deserved, so that you develop their self-esteem.

29   Reward effort and achievement sooner rather than later – don't defer if possible. A quiet word to say well done is probably most effective of all, but you might also explore the use of things like certificates in assembly, a note home to parents in the home/school contact book or reading diary, showing work to other teachers, reading out in assembly, a class good writing scrapbook.

30   Manoeuvre the elements of the hour. Use the literacy hour as appropriate to the teaching points you are making. Sometimes spend half an hour on shared writing. Sometimes start with children writing themselves and then bring them together for the whole-class work. Use the structure of the hour in a planned way that benefits the children. Pay back any time you 'borrow' from other elements, e.g. word level work.

Boys are likely to respond to active and interesting lessons that have been carefully planned and respond to what they can do and what they need to do next. It is clear that we want to raise the achievement of both boys and girls and all the points made above apply to girls as well. It is not the case that all boys are the same. The 30 points listed above are reflected in the snapshots approach described in this book.